PsychoNavigation

PsychoNavigation

TECHNIQUES
FOR
TRAVEL
BEYOND
TIME

JOHN PERKINS

Destiny Books
Rochester, Vermont

Destiny Books
One Park Street
Rochester, Vermont 05767

LIBRARY OF CONGRESS CATALOGING-IN-PUBLICATION DATA

Perkins, John M.
Psychonavigation: techniques for travel beyond time
John Perkins.
p. cm.
ISBN 0-89281-300-8
1. Decision-making--Psychic aspects. 2. Orientation--Psychic aspects.
3. Astral projection. 4. Visualization. 5. Meditation. I. Title
BF1045.D42P47   1990   90-43777
133.8--dc20   CIP

Printed and bound in the United States.

10 9 8 7 6 5 4 3 2 1

Destiny Books is a division of Inner Traditions International, Ltd.

Distributed to the book trade in Canada by Book Center, Inc., Montreal, Quebec

This book is dedicated to Ruth and Jason Perkins who were the first to lead me into other cultures.

Contents

Prologue

My five year old daughter, Jessica, and I stood hand in hand on a hill looking down at the power plant and hydroponic greenhouse. Behind us was a mountain of waste-coal, for years a hazard to the environment and people of this northern Pennsylvania community. Now it would be converted into electricity for local consumption and heat for growing tomatoes; the ash would be used to fill in and rehabilitate old strip mine pits. Due to a technological breakthrough, the burning of the waste would not produce acid rain; in fact, this plant, by replacing older ones, would greatly reduce air pollution.

Jessica squeezed my hand three times, our code for "I love you." I returned four: "I love you too." The sleepless nights, eighty-hour work weeks, and endless days away from home finally seemed worth it. I had set out to prove that a risky, environmentally beneficial project could be financed through conventional, private sources. The $53,381,000 facility we saw spread out below was proof it could be done. It was my gift to Jessica's generation. It was also proof that psychonavigation works.

Twenty years earlier, in 1968, a professor I had at business school told my class: "the theory of supply and demand breaks down where the environment is concerned. Unfortunately, we in the technologically advanced societies assume incorrectly that nature's bounty is infinite. Let me offer a prediction: The survival of life as we know it will depend on decisions your generation makes." He paused. "Please take nature into account as you scale the ladders of corporate America." He went to the blackboard and drew the classical curves for supply and demand. "I suggest you study the non-technologically advanced societies, the primitive ones where supply and demand theory really means something."

Two months after that advice was given, I moved to the Amazon and encountered psychonavigation for the first time. I certainly had

1

no inkling of the long-term impact this experience would have on me. Psychonavigation was little more than a curiosity, and I was a lonely, rather self-centered young man, much more concerned with my own role as a Peace Corps Volunteer in a tiny jungle village than with protecting the environment.

The following pages are, in part, the story of my personal journey of discovery and the ways in which I eventually came to use psychonavigation. In addition, they provide background for a theory of why psychonavigation works and how it is utilized by people from all walks of life: medical doctors, scientists, businessmen, politicians, and artists—as well as mountain mystics and jungle shamans. This book will, I hope, inspire others to become psychonavigators and serve to encourage more extensive research into a subject that offers so many benefits to current and future generations.

One comment I feel obliged to make about authenticity: although the people and incidents are real, in some cases I have changed names and details for the sake of anonymity; conversations are recreated as accurately as memory permits.

My business professor's prediction has come true. The survival of life as we know it depends upon decisions we are making right now. Each year these become more critical. How we live, and the choices we make at the market, at home, and at work affect this planet in ways we are just beginning to understand.

Psychonavigation can enhance our ability to make wise decisions. It can help each of us develop creative solutions to the individual and collective problems we face. Best of all, it can open new worlds of insight and understanding, enabling us to fulfill our obligation as protectors of the Earth.

Before you finish this book, you may want to give psychonavigation a try. I hope so. Once you do, chances are you will make it a part of your life, because it is above all else a truly exhilarating experience.

1

The Road to El Milagro

"Not likely to see any shrunken heads," said Ray, my Peace Corps boss, as he wrestled the wheel of the jeep to bring it through another hairpin turn in the high Andes of Ecuador. Ray was from Atlanta, and he pronounced the words, "shrunken heads," with a drawl that seemed to give them an added measure of respect. It was early morning. The sun had not yet risen, but the massive silhouettes of the surrounding mountains stood out—a haunting landscape against a star-speckled sky. "I dare say you'll meet a few Shuara warriors, but they keep their grisly trophies pretty much to themselves these days."

Because of my degree in business administration, I had been trained at a California camp as a specialist in credit and savings cooperatives. After eight weeks, I was sent directly to Cuenca, a mountain city with a regional Peace Corps office. Ray had offered to drive me to a local market center where I could catch a bus deep into the Amazon. At the end of the road, a horse would take me to my assigned village—El Milagro. It had all seemed very exciting and romantic, but I was beginning to have second thoughts.

"The place you're going to is a frontier outpost, sort of like Dodge City was a hundred and fifty years ago. The only real settlement beyond it is San Miguel, except for Shuara villages."

San Miguel was part of a government colonization effort to move poor mountain peasants deep into the jungle. If they succeeded in clearing and cultivating the land, it was theirs to keep. El Milagro was a key link since it served as a way station for seeds, surveying equipment, and other supplies. Much of this equipment was donated by the U.S. Agency for International Development (USAID) through its Alliance For Progress programs. Peace Corps Volunteers who had been in training with me would help teach these colonists how to survey and farm the jungle.

3

A white wooden cross flashed in front of the headlights; it marked another of the many spots where a driver had lost concentration or control of a vehicle and careened into the icy river hundreds of feet below. I had the impression I was traveling into a land of myths, a place where anything was possible and where the limitations of the world I'd been raised in ceased to exist. The only sound was the jeep's motor, until Ray broke the silence that had crept between us.

"Teofilo Mata is a fine person," he said, never taking his eyes off the road, "Not only El Milagro's schoolteacher, but the town leader, mayor, and council all rolled into one." Ray chuckled dryly. "He understands the importance of a credit and savings co-op. A man of vision! When he asked the Peace Corps to send a Co-op Specialist, he knew what he was doing. Just work with Teofilo, and everything will be A-OK. He'll probably even introduce you to a Shuara or two." Ray leaned forward and squinted through the windshield. "There's Gualaceo now." Ahead, a ghostly light pierced the darkness. "Built a hydro plant here last year. Proud of it they are, too. Runs only a few hours every morning, though, to light the bus station so the Indians can see to set up the market. Terrific assortment of fruits sold here."

"Shuara Indians?" I asked, trying to ignore the apprehension I felt.

"Are you kidding? We're still in the mountains. Quechua country. The Shuara stick to the jungles—except when they psychonavigate."

"Psychonavigate?"

"Yeah. Never heard of it? You will. Happens when a Shaman enters a trance. They say he flies to far off lands. After he returns, he knows things he never knew before. The Quechua psychonavigate too."

"What sort of things does a Shaman learn when he psycho-navigates?"

"You name it," Ray laughed. "They claim he soars on the wings of eagles! I met an old prospector one time—an American named Sam Elliot—who told me a story about how the Shuara found a lost partner of his through psychonavigation. He and his friend had been looking for gold . . . you know, lost Inca cities and treasures—El Dorado. They separated, and when it came time to rendezvous, Sam's friend never showed. Sam waited a day and night. Then went to a nearby Shuara village where he and the shaman were friends. According to what Sam told me, Shuara warriors—wearing nothing but monkey furs and feathers—formed a big circle around the shaman. They chanted and danced. Eventually, the shaman fell into a deep trance. After that he led them to Sam's friend. It took two days and nights. When they found him, he was half dead from hepatitis, but he survived."

"Amazing story!" I peered out the window at the dark, forbidding mountains, once again disturbed by the feeling that I had entered a land where the mythical and tangible are never far apart—if separated at all.

"You'll hear more like it, I'm sure. Remember a few to tell me."

"Do you believe in psychonavigation, Ray?"

He shrugged. "I believe the Shuara found Sam's friend. How? Who knows! Maybe just lucky or good trackers." He slammed on the brakes to avoid hitting a mangy dog. Ahead I saw people congregating in the eerie light of the bus station. "I've been told the Quechua psychonavigate to predict the future. They travel through time. Who am I to knock it?"

Ray pulled up to the bus station. It was a little adobe hut that reeked of diesel fuel.

"That *mixto* over there is yours." He pointed to one of the half dozen dilapidated buses lining the road. "They'll board any minute now. Have fun, I'll see you in a month." He drove off, headed back to Cuenca, leaving me with a terrible, lonely feeling that seemed to settle in the pit of my stomach.

I ambled over to the odd-looking vehicle similar to ones used throughout Ecuador. Mixtos are assembled in local factories by bolting large wooden boxes, like small houses, onto old truck chassis. The outside walls are decorated with rainbow-colored murals, and have rectangular holes cut in them for windows. A small crowd milled around this particular mixto which sported a profusion of psychedelic flowers and a huge sign proclaiming to the world that its name was *Little Flower*.

I stood back trying to avoid the commotion and hide my fear, wishing my six foot frame and curly blond hair didn't stand out so much. Most of the people had the high cheekbones and ruddy features characteristic of the Quechua. They were short, barrel-chested and strong. Several men were busy lashing cargo to the top of *Little Flower* with ropes. Then, at a word from the driver, everyone rushed toward the door. People and animals jostled one another to secure favored places on the hard wooden benches. There were pigs, goats, chickens and roosters, and people of all ages. One man tried to squeeze a rusty bicycle through the door; eventually he and an old woman succeeded in heaving it up to the roof of the mixto where a surly cargo-handler stowed it under a heavy black tarpaulin. I kept off to the side, watching it all and wanting more than anything to be somewhere else.

When the driver saw me, he introduced himself in the sing-song Spanish typical of Ecuador's highlands. "I'm Jaime Ortega, Gringo. This is my bus. I'm the boss here." We shook hands.

"John Perkins, Juan. Pleased to meet you," I lied.

"Mister Juan." A quick smile exposed two gold teeth. "First trip?" He ushered me up the steps of his mixto with much fanfare. Then he stood directly before the family of five crowded onto the front bench. "Make room for this Gringo, so he can see our magnificent country," he said. The eldest son rose and moved to the back of the bus, affording me a space on the coveted front seat. I felt embarrassed and at the same time warmed by such attention. Perhaps things wouldn't be so bad after all.

The six-hour trip was the most spectacular, uncomfortable, and terrifying I had ever taken. We headed into the barren high plains. The *altiplano* is an inhospitable land 14,000 feet up where the air is thin and cold, the vegetation is sparse, and the sun seems to be forever hidden behind massive black clouds—a place designed for phantoms. On the ascent, the inside of the bus was freezing cold. Then we plummeted down into misty jungles. The route was a series of nerve-racking switchbacks, affording first a glimpse of a clouded abyss and then, around the next slippery curve, perpendicular walls of jumbled bamboo, vines, and water cascading into the jungle below. As we descended, the air turned steamy and hot, and *Little Flower's* interior grew so heavy with the smell of sweat that it made me feel nauseous.

Glaring sunshine alternated with torrential rains. The dirt road changed as quickly as the weather. In sunshine, it was a hard-baked surface of bone-rattling ruts; in the rain, it turned to mud. Jaime's driving abilities earned my deepest respect. His job seemed impossible, and yet he was always calm. In fact, he frequently chatted nonchalantly with those of us who sat near. I sometimes found myself wishing he would pay more attention to the road and less to conversation.

Finally, six hours after leaving Gualeceo we arrived at the end of the road. It was not yet noon. Jaime yelled, "Here we are, Highway of the Sun terminal. All out!" Everyone cheered, and I realized with some shock that even seasoned veterans were relieved to have arrived alive.

"Come with me, Gringo." Jaime grabbed my arm and helped me down. My muscles were so stiff, I could barely walk. It felt like the back half of my body was covered with blisters, where my flesh had rubbed against the wooden seat. "Most everyone here is going to the big town of Macas. A short walk. But for you, there is only one way to El Milagro. By horse."

Jamie introduced me to a bearded man with a patch over one eye. "Raul, take good care of this gringo," he said. "Rent him your strongest animal! We want Mister Juan to get the best impression of our magnificent Amazon."

Raul had only four horses and they were all short and scrawny. He led the largest of them to me and accommodated my height by extending the stirrups almost to the ground with rawhide thongs tied to the saddle.

The ride was unlike anything I had ever imagined. The soft jungle soil had been worn down by pack horses and mules to a series of long, deep ditches. Most of the time I could not see over these, although occasionally the horse and I would emerge to a panorama that was magnificent (even to one in my distracted state of mind). This part of the jungle between the Andes and the Amazon's flat flood plains offers splendid views. Vast expanses of rain forest stretch unbroken across endless hills that occasionally rise to jagged peaks. Mist drifts in and out along the ridges and swirls down into the valleys. When the sun shines, it is merciless. Then suddenly it is vanquished by a chilly down-pour. I became accustomed to a dance-like routine performed on the back of a horse, squeezing into a plastic ankle-length poncho; then rushing to struggle free of it. It was the only way to avoid freezing and baking within a matter of seconds.

A few people rode by me on their way from the jungle to the road. Despite what seemed like the harshest of environments, they were full of good humor and their presence helped raise my spirits. Passing was a challenge. One party nudged its animals as high up the embankment as the loose dirt permitted, while the other cautiously inched along the bottom of the ditch. Everyone took a delight in these encounters, calling out greetings, joking, and laughing boisterously.

"Glorious day, ah Gringo?"

"What's a Gringo doing out here in God's Country?"

Although I was plagued by discomfort—blisters from the wooden mixto bench, saddle sores, and severe cramps from what I later learned were amoebas—I found myself bolstered by these encounters, by these poor people who were so full of life.

Mostly I rode alone. During the solitary moments, Ray's story about the shaman haunted me. I tried to recall accounts I had read of the ghost dance and other ceremonies performed by Native Americans. Psychonavigation. Wasn't the thunderbird a symbol of spiritual journeys for various Indian tribes? I daydreamed about the library of boyhood books that was stored somewhere in the cellar of my parents' New Hampshire home.

A sudden wind chilled the air. Leaves whipped at my face, then the rain struck. It beat like bullets against the hood of my poncho. The horse plodded reluctantly along the bottom of the ditch, its hooves splashing noisily in the rising water. A blinding flash of lightning was followed immediately by a clap of thunder.

Just ahead on the left side of the muddy ditch something jerked in the loose mud. Perhaps a lizard or the tail of a rat. Then a flash of color caught my eye: orange, red, and black! A coral snake, deadly poisonous, was sliding down the embankment toward my horse's hooves. My pulse raced as I tried to think of a way out. The ditch was too narrow for turning. If the horse saw the snake, it might rear up and throw me. I began to panic.

The snake slid further down. The horse took another step forward. I tried to calm myself. Searching my memory, I recalled the burning of a neighbor's barn during my childhood, and horses being led out blindfolded. I leaned forward as far as I could and reached around the horse's head, and talked soothingly into one of his ears, cupping my hands over his eyes. With my knees and heels, I gently urged him forward. I forced myself to look straight ahead. His ears twitched, but he plodded steadily on, seeming not to mind, or even notice, that his vision had been restricted. Finally, I allowed myself a backward glance. The snake thrashed in the water at the bottom of the ditch behind me. I sat up and let the breath burst from my lungs. It felt good to know I possessed enough knowledge, or instinct, to get me through such a crisis. The pelting rain seemed almost refreshing.

The cloudburst passed as quickly as it had arrived. Once again, I removed the poncho and stuffed it in my backpack. The horse stumbled upward out of the ditch. At the top, a family of five waited for us to emerge so they could continue on their way to the end of the road. After the usual exchange of greetings, I warned them about the snake and asked, "How far is it to El Milagro?"

The father laughed and pointed along the path behind him. "You're practically there, Gringo. Just beyond that bend."

The trail gradually improved and the increasing frequency of bamboo farm houses with thatched roofs made the time pass more quickly. But it was at least another hour before I reached my destination. And when I did, I couldn't believe my eyes.

El Milagro was less than a dozen tiny shanties framing a muddy plaza no larger than a basketball court. The houses were constructed of primitive, hand-hewn, unpainted boards that ran vertically from ground to roof, spotted with clumps of fungus in varying shades of yellow, orange, and green. There were no windows in the entire village. One building stood out from all the others. It was concrete with a wooden sign in crude red letters that boldly announced it in Spanish as "The El Milagro School, Built with Alliance for Progress Funds." I desperately wanted to turn back; I began to plot my retirement from the Peace Corps, believing there wasn't anything I would not do to avoid living in this squalor.

The horse knew his work was nearly finished. He trotted across the muddy plaza and headed straight for the school. Three naked children and a filthy pig stopped playing to gawk at me. The horse halted so quickly that I had to fight to keep from flying headlong onto a concrete slab that served as a step in front of the building. A scrawny boy watched us over his shoulder. He was facing the schoolhouse and urinating against its wall.

2

Headhunters and the Jaguar-God of the Amazon

A man stepped from inside El Milagro's school onto the concrete slab below. He nudged the boy away with a gentle hand. He stood erect in a rumpled green shirt and unpressed slacks, with hair cropped short, military style. I judged him to be in his mid-twenties, about five feet eight inches or so. Although slim, he possessed the chest and shoulders of the Quechua. My attention was drawn to his shoes. For the first time that day I felt a real urge to laugh. He wore beautiful black dress shoes, with a shine that would make a drill sergeant jealous. How, I wondered, could anyone keep shoes so highly polished in a place like El Milagro? And why? He smiled and stepped gingerly into the mud.

"I'm Teofilo Mata. You must be our new Peace Corps volunteer."

I dismounted. The mud was firmer than it looked. We shook hands. "Yes, I'm here to help you with the credit and savings co-op."

His expression was one of open bafflement. "Credit and savings co-op?" He dropped my hand. "What do you mean? Nobody here has any money." His gesture encompassed the huts scattered around us. "What credit? What savings? You know how it is in El Milagro: My oranges for your bananas, your milk for my eggs. Credit and savings co-op! No, no. There must be some mistake. We need an agronomist for an agricultural co-op."

Teofilo Mata was the only person with a paying job in El Milagro. In 1968, twenty-one pupils attended his school. He taught all grades through the sixth. After that, if a child wanted to continue, the parents had to make arrangements with the school in Macas, several hours to the north.

El Milagro was almost empty of adults from early morning until late afternoon. A few women spent the day in town. Teofilo's wife,

Marta, assisted at the school and baked bread in an outdoor oven in a clearing behind it. Her bread was bartered at the town's "store," a room in one of the houses lining the plaza. Another woman, Eugenia, passed her day tending the store, although the reason for remaining open with so few people puzzled me. Everybody else rose early and headed into the forest. Some harvested fruit. Others collected wild honey. The majority herded cattle or cultivated vegetable gardens on small plots cleared from the jungle. The smell of wood smoke from slash-and-burn agriculture permeated the air. As Teofilo had said, commerce took the form of barter; hard currency was seldom seen.

I moved into the house next to the Mata's. The front rested on the edge of the plaza, but in the back, where the land sloped steeply away to the jungle, the house was supported by eight-foot-high stilts. The side walls were shared with neighbors. Fungus clung to the exposed walls inside as well as outside.

That first afternoon, I carried my backpack and sleeping bag into the single room. Since it had no windows and El Milagro was a very long way from the nearest power line, the only sources of light during the day were the door and a gaping hole in the floor at the back. Upon closer inspection, it was obvious that the floor had never been completed. The boards simply ended about six feet from the rear wall. Looking down through the open space, I saw green slime where a pig foraged for grubs. Beyond was the jungle.

I arranged to pay the Matas a small fee in exchange for meals. Their house was one of the finest in El Milagro, two-storied, perhaps in deference to the role they sometimes played as overnight hosts to the children of parents who were forced to spend the night in the jungle or some distant town. The Matas had a son and daughter of their own.

The downstairs consisted of a single room with three wooden chairs, a bench, and three beds. The second story was divided into two rooms by a split-bamboo wall. One was used for dining; the other for cooking. People living in the jungle who are fortunate enough to have an upstairs locate their kitchens there because they cook over an open stone hearth and the smoke must escape through a ceiling hole. The back wall of the kitchen—the one facing the jungle—had a door, usually open, that led nowhere. There were no stairs outside it; just an eighteen foot drop to the edge of the jungle. The door was used for ventilation and light. In addition, it offered the best view of the jungle in town. Through it, we could see verdant rolling hills, vast expanses of rain forest, occasional flocks of flying birds, and the brilliant azure sky frequently obscured by storm clouds; and we could hear the sounds of the jungle—the shrieking of macaws, the screaming of monkeys, the pelting rain against tropical leaves, thunder, and sometimes at night the distant screaming of a jaguar.

The town's water flowed down through a bamboo pipe from a spring on top of a nearby hill. It emptied into a stone basin near the communal toilets which were considered to be the most modern in this region of the country. Built with Alliance for Progress money at the same time as the El Milagro school, they consisted of four concrete stalls. Each had a hole in the floor. Below, a stream from the hilltop spring washed sewage down the slope into the river east of town. Although the stalls were doorless, they faced the jungle and afforded some degree of privacy.

My attempts at convincing the citizens to form an institution for saving money were, possibly, the funniest things that had ever happened to the people of El Milagro. It was, however, my job and I felt obligated to work hard at it. Against all reason, I spent my evenings talking to them as they returned from the jungle. My speeches were a source of unlimited amusement.

Teofilo was sympathetic and, by nature, kind-hearted. One morning, after breakfast, he took me aside. "We who live in the jungle," he said as he walked me toward his school, "realize that nature knows no failures. We learned this from the Shuara. Everything we do has a result. It may not be the outcome we hoped for; nevertheless it is a result." He squeezed my elbow and led me inside the school room. We sat down across from each other at one of the wooden tables. "Your talks about co-ops are helpful. Our people learn from them. Listen to me when I tell you that El Milagro will not end up with a credit and savings co-op. This is no reflection on you. You will not have failed."

I looked across the table at this man. I knew he must have been extremely disappointed that I had showed up instead of an agronomist. He lived in the roughest of places, yet was so kind and sensitive.

Where had he learned such a philosophy? Suddenly I felt very inadequate. What was I doing in this place? How could I possibly pretend to have anything to offer to these people?

Children began filtering in. I thanked Teofilo for his advice, turned, and headed down the hill towards the river. I heard the roar of the rapids long before reaching them.

The river outside El Milagro is a torrent of glacial waters from the Andes that squeezes through a narrow gorge. In those days, it was impossible to navigate or ford. The only way to reach the opposite bank was by a cable strung from one side to the other suspended some eighty feet above the deafening rapids. To cross, one sat in a tiny box, with legs wrapped around a metal post that anchored this precarious seat to the cable overhead, and pulled oneself hand over hand along the cable to the other side.

For a long while, I sat on the edge staring at the river. Teofilo's words returned. As I watched the water beginning its 2,000 mile journey from the west coast of the South American continent to the mighty Amazon and then on to the Atlantic, I thought about his view of nature. Struggling with the logic of what he had said, I still found it difficult not to feel myself a failure.

Each week El Milagro received a bundle of newspapers from Cuenca. It came by mixto to the end of the road and then by horse. One edition of Cuenca's daily, *El Mercurio*, described a bloody war between the fierce Auca Indian tribe and mercenaries hired by a consortium of international oil companies in the northern jungle, perhaps two hundred miles from us. The article suggested that the Aucas had recruited their own mercenaries, a party of Shuara warriors. There was even a gruesome photograph of a shrunken head. The caption below it read: "Former U.S. Marine Corporal, hero of Vietnam, slain and mummified by Shuara Shaman."

Teofilo was outraged. "Ridiculous! Garbage! That would be sacrilege to the Shuara." He sat down at his desk and scrawled out a letter to *El Mercurio's* editor. Later that afternoon when school was finished, Teofilo invited me to his house. We sat next to the upstairs doorway facing the jungle. His anger had subsided, but he clearly had not forgiven *El Mercurio*.

"The Shuara are remarkable people, Mister Juan. They understand the jungle. It's possible they would fight the oil companies in order to protect the land. But shrink a gringo's head? No! Headshrinking is a religious act. What *El Mercurio* reports is out of the question."

I remembered Ray's story.

"Teofilo, do you know anything about psychonavigation?"

He looked surprised by my question. "Of course." He patted my arm. That too is part of the Shuara religion. They believe God inhabits the souls of animals, especially the jaguar. A Shaman, if properly trained, can become one with the jaguar. The Shuara believe the jaguar actually visits them. It enters their souls and takes them on journeys. It teaches them things. A very direct god."

"Have you seen them do this Teofilo?"

"Yes, many times. I'm part Quechua. I came from SigSig in the Andes. He paused, then gave me an enigmatic grin. "We also psychonavigate. You know, Mister Juan, I'm a good Catholic. A devoted Catholic. Yet, I also see something wonderful in the Shuara religion. When they psychonavigate, I believe they are experiencing a form of enlightenment."

"Sounds like blasphemy, Teofilo."

"No, no. Not at all. I am certain Christ would approve!"

"And the priests?"

He laughed. "A different issue. Living here in El Milagro, my Catholicism has been modified. We see a priest only once every month or two. In between I must rely directly on God and nature." He hoisted one leg over the other and began untying a muddy black leather shoe. "Modern man takes nature too much for granted. We steal from her far more than we need. We are greedy." He removed his shoes. "I have come to see the jungle differently than I once did." He scraped the mud off his shoes with a small pocket knife, letting it fall through the open door.

"Is it being destroyed?"

He stood up and went to a wooden box in a corner of the kitchen. Rummaging around, he pulled out a rag and small metal can. "Certainly at some point there's a limit. But it's an immense jungle." He sat down and dipped his hand into the metal can. When his fingers came out, they were covered with gooey black polish. He rubbed it vigorously on one of his shoes. "I used to think that limit was a long way off. Now I'm not so sure."

"What's changed your mind?"

"Not exactly changed it. Just got me wondering." Meticulously he worked the polish into his other shoe. "The Shuara have acted strangely sometimes. Towards us, you know. They say things about the jungle growing small. Then again, there have been incidents." He buffed the black leather with a rapid movement that caused the rag to crack like a whip.

"What do you mean? What kind of incidents?"

"Only a few months before you arrived, our village was attacked by a jaguar. First it killed a goat out in the Cazorlas' pasture. Then a calf at the Benigno place. Very unusual. Cats are solitary animals; they stay far away from villages. But this one was crazed. We were terrified, especially for our children! We are a mountain people who don't know how to find and kill a jaguar. At night, we lit torches and stuck them in the ground around the town. We avoided the jungle; our outlying gardens and pastures were left untended. Every evening we held a town meeting, but could not agree on a course of action.

"Then four Shuara warriors and their shaman appeared. Nobody sent for them. They just arrived, saying they knew about our problems with the jaguar and had come to help, that the animal was possessed by evil and had to be killed. They wanted to be the ones to do it, as a sacred duty. They also told us the evil had come about because of the way the colonists were treating the jungle." He smiled sadly.

"That night the Shuara permitted us to watch their ceremony. We went down to the river near the cable crossing at sunset and found them already on the far side where they had lit a fire. They had tied the gondola on their side so we couldn't cross. We weren't about to argue, so we sat down and waited. Darkness closed in around us." Teofilo poured us both a cup of coffee. Outside the rain was falling in sheets. Looking through the doorway, I had the impression that I was seated behind a mythical waterfall. The jungle beyond was invisible. He handed me my cup.

"The warriors stood at the four points of the compass around the fire. The shaman sat on a stool next to the fire. Although we couldn't hear them above the roar of the rapids, in the firelight we could see that they were chanting and stamping their feet in rhythm. The shaman sat quietly looking to the east, for them a magical direction, the place where the sun rises and the world begins. Of course, it is also the way into the deepest jungle, home of the jaguar." Teofilo glanced through the doorway and sipped his coffee.

"Their rhythm gradually accelerated. The chanting and stamping grew louder until it reached a frenzy. All the while, that lone figure sat perfectly still on his stool. Then as the rhythm slowed, two warriors danced towards the fire. They picked up the stool and carried the shaman into the darkness. The remaining warriors tossed dirt on the flames. One untied the gondola and sent it back our way. They disappeared into the jungle." He was silent.

"Then what?"

"We walked back up the hill to El Milagro. We all felt relieved, and we talked and joked and sang."

"Weren't you afraid that the jaguar might be lurking in the trees nearby?"

"I don't think that occurred to any of us. We believed in the power of the jaguar-god. We all knew the shaman had joined the god. They had become one. The jaguar in him would lead the warriors to the animal who had terrorized us."

Teofilo stood up in the open doorway. The downpour had stopped suddenly, as if someone had turned off a faucet. The view was now amazingly clear. The jungle stretched end-lessly away, like a thick green fur covering thousands of miles of rugged hills and eventually—beyond our sight—the vast flatness of the Amazon floodplain. I joined him at the door. It gave me an odd sensation to think of the tribes living out there much as they had for thousands, tens of thousands, of years. What did they know that I did not? My own ancestors must have led similar lives long ago. I wondered how much my culture had sacrificed in order to gain material comforts. During that brief moment, it was as if I were somehow drawn by the jungle itself through the doorway into a world I had never experienced but that somehow was part of my genetic makeup.

I looked at Teofilo. He stared straight out over the vast expanse of hills and valleys. It occurred to me that our own existence was a tenuous one. Like the jaguar, the Shuara, and the jungle, all human beings are endangered. It is we who threaten ourselves and we alone who are in a position to do something about it.

Teofilo returned to his seat. With a sense of relief, I turned my back on the jungle and joined him.

"Late the next afternoon," he said, "the Shuara returned to El

Milagro. Two of the warriors carried a pole slung between their shoulders. Hanging from it was a huge dead cat. We have not been bothered by a jaguar since that day."

About a week after Teofilo told me that story, I awoke suddenly one night from a deep sleep, certain I had heard the scream of a jaguar— a chilling scream that reverberated through the jungle into the deepest recesses of my subconscious. For a long time I lay in my sleeping bag thinking about the Shuara and their world. For me the jaguar had come to symbolize that world.

The morning was heavy with fog. After breakfast I sat alone in Teofilo's kitchen, sipping coffee and listening through the open door to the sounds of El Milagro. The adults had left early. On this particular morning all the school children had gone with Marta and several other women to the river. As the fog began to lift, the town became strangely silent. Returning to my house, I took a book from my backpack and sat in the doorway. I could see Eugenia drowsing in a chair at the back of her store. Teofilo was out of sight, probably inside the schoolhouse. The only sounds were the cluckings of a couple of chickens pecking along the edges of the plaza and wandering in and out of a few lingering patches of fog.

I became deeply engrossed in the novel. The sun was soothing and the nearness of the chickens was somehow comforting. Suddenly, without looking up, I knew I was being watched. I felt the presence of the two Shuara warriors before I saw them.

They stood on the far side of the plaza, watching me. They had arrived without a sound and remained there motionless. We looked across the plaza at each other. Around their heads were bands of fur and feathers. Each wore a pair of brown shorts. Their torsos, arms, and legs were bare except for armbands made of leather thongs, feathers, and shells. One carried a blowgun, the other an old single-shot rifle. Their black hair was cropped straight across their foreheads.

Their eyes turned away from me, toward the school. I followed their gaze and saw Teofilo emerging through the doorway.

Wisps of fog drifted in and out of El Milagro. It was very quiet. The place felt smaller, more remote, than ever before. I found myself wondering what the Shuara knew about this village. Had their arrival been planned to coincide with a time when most of the people, even the children, were gone? That seemed impossible. Then it occurred to me that perhaps other warriors lurked in the jungle nearby. The thought sent a chill up my spine. I forced my eyes away from the plaza and searched the fringes of the forest.

Teofilo hesitated, then shouted a word I could not understand. He glanced in my direction, motioned for me to join him, and walked briskly into the plaza.

For an instant I lingered, wondering what I would say to two Shuara warriors, acutely aware that I spoke not a word of their language and only passable Spanish. Teofilo beckoned me forward. The Shuara watched as I walked toward them, their black eyes showing no sign of emotion. When I reached them, Teofilo smiled and introduced us.

"This is Tanya," he said, shaking hands with the warrior who cradled the blowgun. "And," turning to the one with the rifle, "this is Bomi." I shook hands with each, surprised at the lack of firmness in their grips. "My friend Mister Juan is American. Like you, he speaks some Spanish. We will all talk very slowly." This broke the ice. Tanya and Bomi chuckled; they were missing more than a few of their teeth.

"Please," Teofilo said, motioning with both arms toward his schoolhouse. "Let's go in out of the sun. I'll bring beers and something to eat."

"Excuse us." Bomi's Spanish was halting, rather like my own. "But it is nearly noon and we must get home."

"No beer," said Tanya. "We came far to give you a message. We must leave soon. Drink beer, we stay."

"But, you must remain awhile," protested Teofilo." We want to show our friendship. We have not seen our Shuara friends since they killed the evil jaguar."

The two warriors stiffened, their expressions grave. Teofilo did not seem to notice. Bomi lifted his rifle and brought the butt down hard on the ground. "We talk about this spot here."

Teofilo looked puzzled. "This spot?"

"We are sorry," said Tanya. "We do not wish to be rude. But we have important message."

Teofilo peered at each of them carefully. "What, my friends, is this message you bring?"

Tanya nodded at Bomi, who once again raised his rifle and

brought it down hard against the ground. "This spot is the end of colonists' trail. All must stop here in El Milagro." Both warriors stood still looking at Teofilo. The schoolteacher's face was pale. He said nothing.

Tanya lifted his blowgun high over his head and held it parallel to the ground pointing north. "Your colonists must stay on this side of line." With a movement of his head he indicated the west. "They kill jungle, and that must stop."

"But," said Teofilo at last, "Tanya, you know and you too, Bomi, that San Miguel is already out there." He pointed east. "Those are good people. They don't destroy the jungle."

"Yes. Turn jungle to pottery!"

"Pottery?"

"Yes. Must stop here."

"What do you mean 'turn the jungle to pottery'?"

Bomi stepped forward, closer to Teofilo. He looked proudly at Tanya. "My friend is a great shaman. Yes?"

"There is no question about that," agreed Teofilo. "He's the best." It was dawning on me that Tanya was, in fact, the shaman of Teofilo's story whose affinity with the jaguar-god had helped the people of El Milagro before.

"Yes," said Bomi, swelling his chest. "The best." He patted Tanya's shoulder. "Three suns ago, this great shaman was visited by jaguar again."

Teofilo glanced at me. Quickly he looked back at Bomi. "What did the jaguar show this great shaman?"

Bomi turned to Tanya. "Shaman speaks for all Shuara."

Tanya let one end of his blowgun fall to the ground. He rested the weapon vertically against his body. When he spoke, his eyes did not meet ours, but rather looked into the jungle beyond the school house. His voice was deep. Although his Spanish was broken, he never faltered. I was impressed by the authority of his words.

"In early morning, I wake before sun. Climb mountain above river. I dance. Enter land of fathers. I join jaguar-god. He becomes me. Like eagle, jaguar-god flies over forests to land of suns to come. What I see is death. Land is dead. All dead. Trees. Birds. Monkeys. People. Dead. Many, many people. Not Shuara. No. Colonists from mountains, like El Milagro people. Dead. And earth? Burned. Earth like clay after women's fires. Earth is pottery. Earth is dead. And air? Air is smoke. Jaguar-god cannot breathe. Coughing bad. Leave quick. All dead, pottery, smoke. Nothing to do. Only way is way out. Jaguar-god leave. Return to mountain. Talk to warrior, Bomi. Warrior says we must tell El Milagro teacher. Must stop suns to come before they come. We hurry up and tell this fine teacher." He touched Teofilo's arm. "Teacher. He stops colonists before earth becomes pottery. Must stop colonists." He ceased speaking. There was a long silence. A bird's song drifted in from the jungle. Finally, Teofilo cleared his throat.

"You are teacher," Bomi said. "People listen."

"And what if," Teofilo turned to Tanya, "the death wasn't because of the colonists? Perhaps what the jaguar-god saw was caused by a fire."

"No," said Tanya. "Colonists."

"Now," Bomi lifted his rifle to a shoulder. "We go to village. Teacher take care of this." He offered his hand to Teofilo and then to me. We shook hands with them both. Teofilo wished them a safe journey home. I repeated his words. The two warriors turned and walked away. Within seconds they had disappeared into the shadows of the jungle.

Teofilo and I stood together in the plaza. After a while, he shook his head. "Oh my god," was all he said. He walked slowly to the schoolhouse and slumped down on the concrete slab. I sat next to him. He looked totally defeated. Across the plaza, Eugenia stood in the doorway of her store staring into the clump of trees where the Shuara had vanished into the jungle. The chickens continued their pecking along the edge of the row of houses.

I patted Teofilo's shoulder. "You take them very seriously."

"Yes, I do." He rubbed his eyes with the heels of his palms.

"What did Tanya mean about the earth turning to pottery?"

"I guess he thinks farming will destroy the soil, turn it hard like pottery. I've never seen it happen, but the Shuara are seldom wrong about the jungle."

Two weeks after the Shuara visit, the weekly bundle of newspapers from Cuenca contained a note to me from my new Peace Corps boss, Joe. He had replaced Ray and advised me that I was to be transferred to Cuenca. Although I had grown fond of Teofilo and had hopes of spending more time with the Shuara, I was relieved by this news. The fact was that I had nothing to offer the people of El Milagro. I was bored and felt guilty being the only non-productive member of their community. I had petitioned Joe for a transfer.

In all, I had spent nearly six months in El Milagro. I had learned much about the jungle and the people who colonize it. Although I had not seen a jaguar, I had heard its scream at least eight times.

The Shuara did not return during my remaining time in El Milagro. Teofilo told everyone the story about the earth turning to pottery. Otherwise, he did nothing to try to halt colonization. To me, he emphasized the futility of such attempts. "I've told the message of the jaguar-god. What more can I do? After all, who am I to stop such a program?"

The Shuara experience left an impression I would never forget. When I moved to Cuenca, I had several weeks before starting my new job. I spent much of that time talking to people about the Shuara encounter. Joe was not particularly impressed with the jaguar-god; however, he did not discourage me from a brief campaign aimed at persuading Peace Corps and USAID to re-evaluate the colonization program. I wrote letters to the Ecuadorian headquarters of both organizations in the capital city, Quito. I took a grueling seventeen hour bus ride over the dirt road from Cuenca to Quito to discuss this problem with other Peace Corps and USAID co-op specialists at the annual meeting. Before that forum, I presented a paper suggesting that rather than relocating Andean people to the rain forests, we should concentrate on helping them develop new skills and businesses suited to their homes in the mountains. I sent copies of my paper to Peace Corps' world headquarters in Washington, D.C.

For the most part, my petitions were ignored. USAID and the Peace Corps had already established official policies concerning jungle colonization. These were backed by the findings of an impressive array of scientists who had evaluated the environmental impact of the programs. Botanists, zoologists, geologists, agronomists, and biologists had all concluded that small-scale resettlement projects like San Miguel, were compatible with rain forest ecology. I was reminded that this was merely the latest in a long line of traditions growing out of nineteenth century U.S. policies including the Homestead Act.

Although a few other Peace Corps volunteers had expressed concerns about possible ecological disruption, our voices were weak. We lacked conviction. We pointed out to each other that we had not actually witnessed any ill effects from colonization. We were guided not by scientific principles, but rather by intuition and the visions of one Indian Shaman. Meanwhile, many of our friends— volunteers from Dayton, Staten Island, and Portland—risked their lives in the steamy jungles to help starving peasants build a new future. According to the scientists, the benefits of colonization outweighed the few harmful effects that might reasonably be expected to occur even under the worst of circumstances. Our campaign fizzled.

It was not long, however, before the scientists were proven dreadfully wrong. The botanists, geologists, agronomists and biologists had made terrible, irreparable miscalculations. The jaguar-god's prediction came true.

San Miguel and other colonization sites had to be abandoned. The problem was that the rain forest turned out to be much more fragile than anyone had imagined. Anyone, that is, except the Shuara and perhaps other "uneducated" tribes. Once the trees were cut, there was nothing to hold the topsoil in place. As soon as the thin network of roots rotted and the rainy season began, the soil was washed down the barren slopes and swept away by the swirling waters of swollen rivers. Beneath the topsoil, there was only clay.

After the rainy season was over, the sun baked the clay hard. Where colonists had cleared the trees and cultivated a harvest or two of vegetables, all that was left to memorialize their efforts were scorched plots of cracked dried earth, hard as bricks. Tanya's "suns to come" had arrived. The earth was dead; turned to pottery.

3

Don Quischpe, Incas, and the *Kon-Tiki* Voyage

Cuenca is a city of 120,000 inhabitants high in a mountain valley just south of the Equator. Colonial sections date back to the early sixteenth century. White adobe buildings are decorated with intricately carved wooden balconies and red tiled roofs. Many streets are cobblestone. There are more than a dozen colonial churches, including a central cathedral with an interior of Italian marble. On any given weekend a visitor is likely to find a concert or fiesta in at least one of the city's twenty plazas.

Although the region around Cuenca is populated primarily by Indians, city politics are controlled by descendants of the Spanish conquistadors, the *buena gente*. The buena gente also own most of the businesses.

When the Peace Corps transferred me from the Amazon to the high Andes, it also decided I should work with production rather than credit and savings organizations. My new job was to help a brickmakers' cooperative implement sound management practices and develop markets for its products among the construction companies owned by the buena gente.

The brickmakers themselves were Quechua Indians who lived in Sinincay, a small village an hour away by truck over bone-jarring roads into the mountains west of Cuenca. Teofilo had told me that Quechua psychonavigate, and I found the prospect of working with people from this ancient civilization exciting.

"Quechua" is used to denote members of a large population of Indians living in Ecuador, Peru, and Bolivia; although historically their roots spread to a number of distinct cultures, they were all organized under the rule of the Inca, and today speak one of the

23

Quechua language dialects. The co-op was managed by Josélito Jesus Quischpe.*

After several months of testing each other, Don José (as he was known by co-op members) and I became friends. He was a descendent of the mighty warriors who fought in the Incan armies against the conquistadors. Proud of his heritage, he was flattered by my interest in the history of his people.

Don José rose before the sun. Each day, after a quick breakfast with his wife and four children, he and his oldest son, Manolo, and daughter, Maria, left their single room adobe house near Sinincay and hurried down a precipitous trail that wound around tiny plots of land owned by brick-making families, past young boys hauling eucalyptus branches up to the doors of the brick kilns, and girls hard at work molding clay into bricks of various shapes and sizes. They might exchange greetings with one or two of the fathers who either stacked clay bricks already dried in the sun into the kilns, or hauled the fire-cured red bricks out through the tops of the ovens and loaded them onto trucks.

Don José and his two children waited beside the dusty road until the first truck pulled alongside. It did not matter whether it was carrying a co-op member's bricks or those of a competitor; it would stop. The family riding on top of the stacked bricks would help Don José and his children up, and the truck would resume its journey to Cuenca.

About an hour after leaving their house, the Quischpes arrived at the co-op's warehouse in Cuenca. Usually Maria and Manolo spent a half hour or so helping their father tidy up before leaving for school.

The warehouse was a dirt yard, about a half acre in size, surrounded by a high adobe wall. The side facing Sucre Street had a wooden gate large enough to accommodate the largest of the trucks. Next to the door was a wooden shed. Inside the shed were a table and three chairs and a bare light bulb suspended from the ceiling; this was Don José's office.

My first months at the co-op coincided with the rainy season. Don José and I spent many hours inside his office. I taught him about

---

*For a detailed description of the Sinincay co-op and its manager see John M. Perkins, *The Stress-Free Habit* (Rochester, Vermont: Healing Arts Press, 1989), Chapter 5.

accounting and inventory control. He explained the intricacies of the brick business to me. Sometimes I tried to help him understand what Miami, Boston, or New York were like. He told me about the Quechua. In the high Andes, even during the rainy season, the sun can be very strong. When the rain stops, the ground dries quickly. The sky turns a vivid blue. It is a custom that when the downpour ceases, even for a few minutes, people migrate from inside their homes, shops, and offices out onto the streets. They stroll to a favorite sidewalk café, take a turn around the nearest plaza, or simply wander outside to chat with a neighbor.

One afternoon, as we sat inside, Don José told me about the Quechua gods.

"Hear the thunder? That is Ilyapa. The earth is Pachamama. The moon, which we will see in all her glory tonight, is Mama Kilya. And of course all things were created by the only creator, Viracocha." He looked at me and cocked his head. "Have I never told you about the beginning of the Incas?" He stood up and pointed through the open door.

"See, the rain has stopped. Inti, the sun, has once again smiled on the Quechua as he did so many hundreds of years ago." He patted my back. "Not really so long ago. You and I were comrades then as we are now." He laughed and ushered me through the door.

Together we stood in the yard and looked up over the wall at the top of a nearby peak. The sun's light reflecting off it turned its volcanic face to orange. I followed Don José through the gate out onto Sucre Street. He stopped. "Viracocha had created men and women many thousands of years before. However, poor creatures that we were, we made little progress. We lived in caves. All we ate were wild berries and animals we killed with our bare hands." He looked away from me, down the cobblestone street toward the Tomebamba River. "Look, there." He pointed at the Indian women who washed clothes for the buena gente. Some stood knee deep in the freezing waters flowing from Andean ice fields to the Amazon, their long skirts tucked up between their thighs. Others lugged bundles of clothing along the banks. Some were struggling to hang freshly washed linens in the branches of nearby bushes. "They work very hard." His eyes met mine. "They still count on Inti to help them, as do all the brickmakers. We always let the sun dry our bricks before firing them in our ovens.

"Inti looked down and, seeing that people lived like beasts, decided to take pity. He summoned his own son, Manco Capac, and his wife, Mama Ocllo. 'Go down to earth,' he commanded. 'Teach men how to build villages and raise crops.' He gave them a golden staff as long as" Don José spread his arms wide "a condor's wings, and told them to throw it at the ground a hundred times each day. 'When it sinks into the earth,' Inti said, 'You will know you have arrived. This is where you must build a city. A kingdom of light and wisdom will sprout from the golden staff and you will rule this kingdom.'

"Manco Capac and Mama Ocllo were delighted by these words. Then Inti grew stern. 'You must always remember,' he warned, 'You are the protectors. You must teach this to your children and they to their children. You have a great responsibility, for you are my servants. You are guardians of all my children, of plants and animals and all that has been put upon Pachamama. Your kingdom is a kingdom of people. You are the rulers of people and of people alone. The rest—plants, animals, Panchamama herself—fall under your protection, but not your rule. Remember this well and see to it that all your children and all their children obey this law; above all other laws, this is the most important. Cultivate farm lands to satisfy your needs. No more. Build cities to house your people and to worship Viracocha, Mama Kilya, and the other gods. But not a building more. Heed this well, my children.' And with those parting words, he left them."

Down by the Tomebamba, the Indian women continued washing the clothes of Cuenca's buena gente. It occurred to me that tons of soap must flow each year from Cuenca into the Amazon. But this, I knew, was nothing compared to the pollution caused by my own country and other industrialized nations throughout the world. For an instant I no longer saw the cobblestone street with washerwomen standing knee-deep in a river at its end. Instead I saw Los Angeles freeways, Boston harbor sewage, and the New Jersey industrial wastelands just outside New York City. Perhaps things would be different, I thought, if we were all brought up with myths like those of the Quechua. I glanced up. Don José was peering at me. "What do the Quechua think of the world today?" I asked.

He too looked towards the Tomebamba. "We wonder why Inti

allows some things to happen. As for me, you know I often read the paper. I learn that some people try to rape Pachamama. I cannot understand this. The earth, the air and water, the trees, flowers, and animals are all we have. Are not these people smart enough to comprehend this? And why does Inti allow the destruction to go on? I often ask Inti. I pray and meditate. I have not yet received an answer. But I can say this: The Quechua still follow the edict. We are protectors, not destroyers. The problem is we are very few and we are not the warriors we once were. How do we stop all the others, those who humiliate Pachamama?"

One day I told Don José about El Milagro and my attempts to form a credit and savings co-op in a town with a barter economy. He was greatly amused. After a good laugh, he wiped the tears from his eyes. As he did so, he removed the Panama hat he always wore. It was one of the few times I ever saw the top of his head. The Andean Indian and his hat are inseparable.

"You know," Don José said as he smoothed down his thick black hair and replaced the hat, "it wasn't so long ago that my people lived without knowledge of money. The Incas built magnificent highways and fortresses. They terraced steep slopes into fertile agricultural plots. They were great mathematicians, warriors, and organizers of people. And yet, they had no money.

"The Inca System was one that did not require currency. All food was stored in vast warehouses. It was given to the people. No person went hungry or lacked shelter. Clothes and medical care were provided, no one bought anything. The sick, the old, the insane were cared for by agents of the king. But no one—not even the king himself—had money. It was not exactly a barter system, like El Milagro's, but it was one that did not depend on money."

"What about all that Inca gold?"

"Ah, yes. There was much gold. Beautiful ornaments and statues. But it was all owned by Viracocha, Inti, or one of the other gods. The king—who after all was himself part god—was allowed to wear it. He could lend gold, silver, and precious stones to others, but only for spiritual purposes, for religious ceremonies, to honor the gods or request their services. You see, despite all the capabilities possessed by my ancestors—as scientists, administrators, soldiers, artisans, and farmers—what they valued most was their spirituality. They communicated directly with the gods. They listened to inner voices. When Viracocha or Inti spoke, they obeyed. And they still do."

"Have you ever heard of psychonavigation, Don José?" I briefly explained what I had learned from Tanya and Teofilo. He listened attentively. When I finished, he pushed his chair away from the table.

"Yes. What you describe, I think, is a Spanish concept stolen from a Quechua religion."

I related to him the story of El Milagro's jaguar. He stood up and looked out the doorway into the warehouse yard.

"The Quechua are as different from the Shuara as your people are. But the incident you relate is not unlike things we experience." He turned to face me. "One day perhaps you can participate in a Quechua ceremony where what you call 'psychonavigation' happens." Behind him, a truck carrying bricks drove into the warehouse, its horn blaring loudly. Don José reached for his inventory book. "Now we have work to do."

He hurried to the truck. I joined in, close on his heels, shaking hands with the family who had dug the clay, molded it into bricks, baked and loaded them and traveled down the rough road from Sinincay on top of their precious cargo. Juan José Chuqui was the co-op president. He and his brother, Julio Mora Chuqui, had brought their wives, three teenage girls, and two boys. Without fanfare, they began unloading. Three people remained in the truck. They stacked the bricks into piles and handed them down to those on the ground, who carried them off to different areas indicated by Don José. Normal size bricks were allocated to one section of the yard; gigantes, the extra large ones, to another. Roofing tiles were stacked near the door. I assisted Don José at tabulating the numbers and characteristics of each type of brick.

For Juan and Julio Chuqui and their families, it was back-breaking work. Within minutes, the warehouse was obscured in a cloud of brick dust. The bricks were heavy and jagged. These people had been working since dawn. Only this morning they had hauled the bricks out of the ovens and onto the truck. They had eaten a breakfast of bread, potatoes, and fruit while riding atop a pile of bricks in the back of the rickety truck descending a precipitous and pock-marked dirt road. And yet here they were, good-naturedly bantering with each other as they lugged their unwieldy loads across the yard. There was constant laughing and joking among them. Frequently, one would slap playfully at another as they passed.

These people had been exploited for centuries. They were paid very little for their toil. Traditionally, the Quechua brickmaker earned barely enough to survive, while the buena gente middlemen and the architects and engineers profited handsomely. Although the co-op was an attempt to redistribute the wealth in a more equitable manner, its effectiveness had not yet been proven.

Watching these people and the way they interacted with each other, I could not help but be impressed. But there was another feeling, difficult to define. Was I possibly jealous of this Quechua family? There was no denying that I who had never known poverty or hunger felt, if not jealousy, at least envy for their ability to enjoy so completely each other, their work, the meager food and homes they shared, and all that was around them. I had learned that Andean Indians often talk to nature. It is not uncommon to hear a man or woman murmur words of greeting to a bird, flower, or cloud. Such things are a part of their lives and the source of immense pleasure. I found myself recalling the discussion Don José and I had just concluded. His comments about the Quechua views of nature and spirituality took on added meaning. Was it possible that these people knew something my ancestors and I had forgotten? I felt drawn towards something I did not understand. Here in the Cuenca warehouse, it seemed less threatening than it had in El Milagro. Don José's suggestion that I too might participate in psychonavigation had sent a wave of excitement through me. Could I learn from the Quechua what my own background and culture had failed to teach?

The Chuquis completed their work in a little less than two hours. Don José prepared a line at the bottom of his tally sheets for the two brothers to sign. We all shook hands. It began to rain about the time they were preparing to climb back into the truck for the return trip to Sinincay, and I suggested we all try to squeeze into the office.

"Oh no," one of the women said in halting Spanish. "We love showers." She held her mouth open, raised her head, and cupped her hands under her chin. I glanced around to see that several other family members were doing the same thing. Two of the girls were dancing.

The boys had rigged a tarpaulin into a tent over the fence-like slats at the front of the truck bed. The others climbed up to sit under this. As the truck roared through the gate into Sucre Street, they waved and shouted happily. We could hear them singing after the tailgate had disappeared behind an adobe wall.

The rain ended shortly after noon, the time most Cuencanos begin their daily siesta. The city virtually closes down for about two hours so families can relax together. Since it was not possible for Don Jose to travel to Sinincay and back in two hours, he usually kept the warehouse open. Although sales to engineers and construction companies were never made during the siesta, once in a while small lots were sold and carted away on a man's back or in a wooden wheelbarrow.

"No business for a while," Don José said. "Not after a rain like that. See how Inti shines now! Nobody will come for a couple of hours." He patted me on the shoulder. "Let's go down by the river and talk about psychonavigation."

He snapped the fist-sized padlock shut on the warehouse gate and we headed toward the Tomebamba. Up river, colonial homes gleamed in the sunlight. They clung to the edges of rocky cliffs out over the swirling water. We were nearly a half mile away, but even at this distance, the intricately carved wooden balconies stood out in relief against the white adobe background of the sixteenth century walls. Don José led me to a stone bench. We sat down. Indian boys wearing blue ponchos and miniature Panama hats played soccer on the steeply sloping bank. Our bench was shaded by a tree. Next to it, marble steps descended to the ruins of an ancient foot bridge washed away in a forgotten flood.

"There are many stories about what you call 'psychonavigation,'" Don José said. "One that reminds me of your jaguar experience concerns Tupa Inca, a king who ruled before Huayna Capac, the father of Atahuelpa. Word had come to him in Quito that strange men had landed at a place on the Pacific coast in boats that looked like spiders. Tupa Inca arrived with his army and priests at this spot, near the town known today as Salinas. No one had seen anything like the sight awaiting them. More than a hundred men were camped in the trees above the beach. They were black and their blackness could not be washed away. Along the water's edge was a line of boats unlike anything they had seen before.

"The foreigners spoke a language that none of Tupa's people could understand. After several days, one of the Inca priests made a breakthrough using sign. He learned that these men had come from a faraway land. They had sailed their boats for many days before becoming lost and disoriented in a violent storm. The sea, they said, had risen into huge whirlpools towering up to the heavens. Boats had been sucked up by the sky gods and vanished forever. On the morning after the storm, the survivors peered through the haze toward the rising sun. What they saw terrified them. An army of giants was massed across the horizon shutting out the sunrise. The shadows cast by these monsters enveloped them. They were so frightened they could do nothing. They were powerless. They could not return home, for they had neither food nor water; besides, they had totally lost their bearings. They drifted at sea, hopeless.

"Eventually the sun rose over the giants. In the afternoon, with the sun at their backs, the foreigners recognized their folly. There were no giants, only land. These people had never before seen mountains like the Andes, that stretched from horizon to horizon and blotted out the morning sun. Once they understood what they were seeing, they put their boats to shore."

Don José rose from the stone bench. One of the boys playing on the river bank had missed a pass; the soccer ball bounced up the marble steps. Don José expertly kicked it back, then returned to his seat.

"Tupa Inca was impressed by the bravery and skills of these black people who had traveled so far. Through sign, his priest told them that the Inca was king of the world. He would show them the way home if they promised to give him gifts and name their land after him. They, of course, agreed.

"Tupa Inca ordered his high priest to psychonavigate to the home of these dark strangers. A splendid ceremony was held. There were feasts with music and dancing. At the end, the Incan warriors formed a large circle. In the middle was a gold staff, symbolic of the one given to Manco Capac and Mama Ocllo by Inti. As the warriors stamped their feet and chanted, the priest, clothed only in the feathers of a bird, danced in a circle around the gold staff. The chanting continued for hours. The priest danced and danced. At first he sang; then his words became squawks. His arms turned to flapping wings. Suddenly, he disappeared. He was missing for days.

Eventually he returned in his human form. He spoke to no one until he met with Tupa Inca. 'I have visited their land,' he said. 'It is a beautiful island. I will guide you to it.'

"Tupa Inca ordered his commanders to have many rafts built. They were told to prepare one thousand of the best warriors for a Pacific crossing. They fashioned a special raft for Tupa Inca and his priests. On the appointed day, they set sail. Oh, what a magnificent sight! It is said that people from all over the kingdom—from what is now Chile, Bolivia, Peru, and Colombia—journeyed to the Ecuadorian coast to bid farewell to their ruler.

"It was ten moons before they saw him again. Some feared he would never return. But he did. He came back to the exact spot from where he had left, he and all his priests and warriors. Their rafts were piled high with gifts: hundreds of carved stones, bracelets, necklaces, even a magnificent stone throne for Tupa Inca."

He touched my knee with his hand as he stood up. "Come. Let's head back to the warehouse. For me and my people—stories of psychonavigation are simply part of our history. People still psychonavigate. Given the proper motivation and desire, anyone can do it."

This was what I had waited to hear. "When can I see it, Don José? Who do you know that psychonavigates?"

"Have you ever heard of the Birdmen of the Andes? One day I will take you to them."

During more than two years in the Andes, I came across many reports of psychonavigation experiences. The Tupa Inca story was related to me on several occasions, in essentially the same form.

From time to time I tried to discover who the black people really were and whether in fact there was an island in the Pacific named "Tupa Inca" or "Inca" or "Tupa" or "Inti" or something that remotely resembled a word that would help authenticate this story. But it wasn't until the late 1970s that the story was confirmed for me, in an article about the modern explorer, Thor Heyerdahl, and his sailing raft, *Kon-Tiki*.

Heyerdahl wanted to demonstrate that South American Indians could have crossed the Pacific by raft. In 1947 he built and skippered a balsa log raft, that set sail from Callao, Peru, to the amusement of many scientists. On its 101st day from shore, *Kon-Tiki* did indeed land on a coral-reefed island 4,300 nautical miles from its launch.

Among the Polynesian islands, about where Heyerdahl guessed other navigators might have landed such rafts, is a coral reef with a passage still called Teava-o-Tupa. This reef encircles the island of Mangareva, where Heyerdahl discovered legends of rafts carrying a thousand soldiers that came to shore. The tradition says that Chief Tupa once came with a fleet of rafts from a vast and populous land. Even as recently as the last century, the Mangareva lagoon sheltered big rafts that sailed to far islands and returned. Today the people of the island use the same word for potato as did the Incas when Pizarro arrived in the Andes.*

But this information was still far in my own future, and only the press of work helped to pass the time until Don José would act on his promise to take me to the Birdmen of the Andes.

---

*For a detailed account see L. McIntyre, *The Incredible Incas and their Timeless Land* (Washington, D.C.: National Geographic Society, 1975).

4

Birdmen of the Andes

The brickmakers' co-op had existed about seven months when the Peace Corps assigned me to it. Only five families—all from Sinincay—had joined.

The members at first were very suspicious of my motives. They had never heard of the Peace Corps. What was I gaining? How was I paid? One day, while riding on top of a load of bricks being trucked down a winding mountain road, a small group gathered around me. What was the name of my god, they wanted to know. And when would I start persuading them to convert?

Two of the families took every possible opportunity to assure me that there was no gold on their property and that if I succeeded in taking land from them, I could expect little reward—only the hard work of a brickmaker!

Needless to say, I worked diligently to dispel their fears. I attended their *fiestas*, ate and got drunk with them. Several times each month I borrowed films from the Cuenca U.S. Information Agency office, along with a jeep, projector, and generator from the Peace Corps, and showed films outdoors against the side of a Sinincay adobe house.

One time is especially vivid. Don José had ridden in the jeep with me through Sigchio, a neighboring town, and out to an area where there were a dozen or so remote brickmaking operations. I had a megaphone and Don José used it to announce to the community that a documentary about the recent Apollo moon landing would be shown in Sinincay. It must have struck some of those Quechua families as rather odd to see Don José's head thrust through the window of a passing jeep, a megaphone protruding from his mouth like a giant proboscis. He was generally a quiet, sincere man, very reserved and not at all prone to drawing attention to himself. I could not help recalling the itinerant circuses that traveled the small towns of New England during my boyhood summers and the "come-one, come-all" barkers who lured us to the big top with promises of spectacles so bizarre they excited the imaginations of everyone.

Later that evening I began to sense the level of interest in the film when I saw the numbers of people congregating even before I had finished setting the projector up on the jeep's hood. Julio Chuqui and his eldest son, Luis, helped me uncoil the long electric cord and trail it from the projector down into the dry ravine behind their kiln where we had positioned the noisy generator. It took longer than usual to start the machinery. After tugging the flywheel rope for several minutes to no avail, I stood back exhausted. Luis offered to take over.

Clambering out of the ravine, I was astounded by the sight confronting me. Sinincay was a tiny town of eight adobe houses and several brickmaking facilities, located at the bottom of a natural amphitheater. The sides were barren hills rising to the higher mountains. Standing where I was, practically in the center, I looked up. From every side, down all the hills, descended dozens of Quechua families. They swarmed into the space between the jeep and the side of the house where the movie images would appear. The sun was low and the air turning chill. It would be a cold night. On they came, men, women, and children, wrapped in heavy ponchos and woolen blankets. Some of the women carried sleeping babies strapped to their backs. I was amazed to discover that so many families lived in the mountains around Sinincay and that all of them, it seemed, had come to see my movies.

I stood there alone, awed and somewhat frightened. What did these people expect? How far had they walked? What if they were disappointed? I had brought only two films: the moon landing, and a propagandistic one about the importance of working together in cooperatives.

The sun disappeared below the dusky mountains. A silver edge of the moon peaked over the roof of the house in front of me—on the equator, daylight does not linger. Behind, I heard Luis cursing as he cranked away at the generator. The long shadow of night spread over Sinincay. A tiny light flickered on in the hills, then another. Soon they appeared all around us, golden imitators of the stars above. Quechua lanterns and candles moved along hidden trails as brickmakers continued to find their way into the plaza. Luis cursed again. It occurred to me that I should find him a light. Then a sense of panic gripped me. What if the generator was broken?

A lantern came toward me from out of the darkness. Above it, I saw first the hat brim, then the forehead and eyes of Don José. "A good crowd," he said softly. "Our megaphone trip was a big success. You know, after you last showed this moon film, we who saw it told the others. Everyone wanted to see it. I'm pleased so many were able to come."

"Uh huh," I said. I reached out and gripped his shoulder. "The generator worked last week. Another volunteer took it to his village. He told me it worked fine."

"What?" Don José yelled. I suddenly realized that our voices had been drowned by the explosive clatter of the generator, working at last. With a euphoric sense of relief, I led Don José away from the ravine. "Never mind. Let's get this movie started."

"But they're still coming. Can't we wait a little while?"

The moon shone silver bright and almost full above the house that served as our screen. In the cold, thin air, she seemed to reach down to us. I understood why the Incas had worshipped silver as the moon's tear drops. Mama Kilya was alive to me this night. I could feel her presence. She seemed very close, and there was an energy emanating from her—not the physical energy we feel from the warmth of her consort, Inti, the sun, but a spiritual energy, one of mystery, inner discovery, hope, and redemption. Everyone in that plaza was facing her. Were they waiting for the movie to appear or were they silently offering homage to Mama Kilya?

Don José touched my elbow. "Okay," he said, "everyone is here."

I flicked the switch. The side of the adobe house was flooded in light. A Spanish voice boomed through the speakers. We all watched as NASA prepared its rockets and the men who would fly them.

I walked behind the jeep, toward the ravine, and listened. The generator seemed to be running smoothly. I stood there all by myself in the pitch black night, feeling like an astronaut on a strange, wild and wonderful journey, a man who had brought electricity, movies, and the story of the Apollo landing to people who still lived much as they had centuries ago under the Inca; for many of them it was the first film they had ever seen. I felt wonderfully happy. I wanted to be close to these people.

Returning to the projector, I was treated to a scene of incredible beauty and power. The Quechua congregation, bundled in their woolen ponchos, were huddled together in the tiny square on that cold Andean night. Not a soul spoke. They stood in speechless awe, their attention riveted to the side of the neighbor's house where a rocket hurtled toward the silver orb that the men in the rocket called the moon, and the Quechua worship as Mama Kilya.

That splendid, shining globe was poised above the wall, above the rocket and the moon on the wall, above the Quechua spectators who sat mutely watching the projected images, above the projector, the generator, the jeep, and the village of Sinincay. She hung there crystal clear in the dark heavens and looked down at us all as we looked from her to her image on the wall, and back again.

"Mama Kilya." Don José spoke the name quietly. Around him, I heard many voices reverently echo his words.

Don José became my ally. He was the closest to me and was the first to understand that I had something to contribute; he knew that I was taking nothing from the co-op in return. Occasionally we visited other projects where the Peace Corps was involved. As he taught me about his world, he began to comprehend mine. We shared a common trait that helped to seal the bond between us: circumstances had placed each of us in a foreign culture. Cuenca and its buena gente previously had been as unknown to him as the Quechua had been to me. His growing faith spread to the others. They knew and trusted him, and I could see that as his trust in me grew, so too did membership in the co-op. During the tenth month after my arrival, we welcomed in our tenth family.

Every month the members of the co-op met in Sinincay. For eleven months I stood before their meetings and summarized the progress I was making. I listed the names of the buena gente with whom I had met and to whom we hoped to sell the co-op's bricks without the extortion of middlemen. I outlined my strategy for the following month. But as the year grew shorter, my confidence diminished. It was common knowledge that the buena gente would not negotiate with a Quechua. As a gringo, I had thought I could surmount this obstacle. The fact was, I had been admitted to buena gente social circles. I sipped coffee at sidewalk cafés with Cuenca's elite. I was invited to their lavish parties. I tutored their children in English. I wrote recommendations to U.S. universities. But I signed no contracts. At the twelfth co-op meeting I felt sick at heart. I stood up and apologized. I had lived the good life in Cuenca while these people had slaved in their clay pits and primitive ovens. And I had failed them.

After that meeting, Don José led me outside. Together we walked to the top of a knoll and looked down on Sinincay's dusty plaza.

"The Spanish conquistadors were sent here by the Creator, Viracocha, to teach the Quechua a lesson," Don José said. "In his zeal to expand his father's empire, Atahualpa had slain his brother, Huascar. The Quechua rulers and their people had lost sight of the laws laid down by their ancestors. Viracocha was furious. He told Atahualpa that men wearing suits of sunlight would be sent to teach the Quechua a lesson. 'You must obey my commands,' Viracocha said. 'Listen to your ancestors. Open your hearts to them and do as they tell you. Their words are mine.' Before his death, Atahualpa spread Viracocha's message throughout the realm: the Quechua must always follow the commands of the ancestors."

We watched as a little girl struggled to raise a bundle of wood to her back. She tied the leather thongs around her shoulders, then shuffled off toward the distant mountains we could see far on the other side of the Tomebamba valley. A tiny spire in the hazy distance between the little girl and the mountains was the only sign of Cuenca and its Catholic churches.

Don José placed a hand on my shoulder. "You must have faith," he said. "At the meeting you were hard on yourself."

"I haven't much time. You always say I should be patient. Well, as you know my days here grow short."

The hand on my shoulder turned me slowly to face him. "I never told you this before," he said, "but it was at the ceremony of the Birdmen that the ancestors commanded me to start the cooperative. There will be a ceremony next week. Will you please join me this time?"

I could hardly believe what I was hearing. "You mean the psychonavigators?"

He smiled gently. "Yes. Now you will have your chance to see psychonavigation in person. But," he held up a finger, "I won't take you simply to satisfy your curiosity. Something greater will occur."

"Faith is like the mortar holding a wall together." Don José's words seemed to take on renewed vigor with every mile we drove into the dark mountains. "You don't need to believe in my religion to understand this. Rituals mean little, unless they help open the heart. That is important. Open your heart. Listen to it and follow its commands. Have faith in what your heart says. Without the mortar of faith, even the sturdiest wall will collapse."

We had left before dawn, headed for a town more than two hours further into the Andes than Sinincay. I drove a Peace Corps jeep over roads that sometimes were marked only by horse droppings. Hail slashed against the windshield. Occasionally our headlights exposed an Indian hut or a pack of dogs. Don José shared the seat next to me with two children. In the back were his wife and another co-op member, that member's wife, and three children. Few words were spoken, except for exchanges between Don José and me on the subject of faith. He had shrugged off most of my questions relating to how it was possible for men to fly with responses like "You will see soon enough" and "It is faith."

The air not only was cold; it was thin. The altitude was higher than anything I had experienced in recent months. I began to feel light-headed. "Can the Birdmen fly only in villages this high up?"

Without looking away from the road, I could feel his eyes. "That has nothing to do with it. You really don't understand, do you? Flying is not just physical; it is also spiritual. I can't tell you about it. You have to experience it. Your experience may be different from mine. Remember this as you watch. When the Birdmen fly, it is to seek advice from dead ancestors. Atahualpa decreed: we must obey God's commands as related through our ancestors. These things are not to be understood, only felt. Perhaps you will feel them as we do. Who knows?"

When we pulled into the village I could see from my watch that the sun should have risen. Yet the morning was dark. The hail had turned to a cold drizzle; fog blanketed the dirt plaza. Occasionally, huts appeared, like phantoms, through the fog.

Don José pointed to one of the huts. It was next to the plaza and slightly larger than its neighbors. I parked the jeep in front of it. A crude cross was painted in red above the door. As I turned off the engine I became aware of the dancers.

First I heard the slow beating of a drum. Then the shrill notes of bamboo flutes. I stepped from the jeep into the rain. They materialized out of the fog. Their huge wings flapped in rhythm with the drum, faces hidden by furry masks. The Birdmen. Dressed in skins and feathers—foxes, deer, and condors—they danced in an undulating circle. Their heads swiveled from side to side; above the eye-slits in their masks were the faces of animals whose mouths were agape as though frozen in a moment of inexplicable horror.

The Birdmen danced around two poles painted gold and crossed on the ground. I recognized them immediately as symbolic of the staff given to Manco Capac and Mama Ocllo by Inti—just like those in the ceremony performed by Tupa Inca's priest before his flight over the Pacific! From time to time one of the Birdmen would shriek—the sound of an enraged eagle—and breaking from the circle, rush at the cross. At the last moment he would spread his wings to their full extent, leap, and glide high above the poles to land on the ground opposite and rejoin the circle.

I felt as though I were standing next to Tupa Inca himself, watching a ceremony that occurred long before the first Spaniard set foot in the Americas. The primitive music of drum and flute, the dancers, the very fog itself mesmerized me. I lost all sense of time. I spoke to no one.

A breeze slowly swept the fog from the plaza. Several dozen Indians were standing outside the circle. Huddled beneath somber ponchos, they too seemed lost in the world of the dancers.

When I glanced at my watch I was surprised to see that I had been transfixed by this ceremony for nearly two hours. None of the dancers had rested. Their amazing stamina and the energy of their flights across the poles convinced me that I was witnessing an event that transcended normal human abilities. I felt that these men had in some sense left us to enter into other worlds.

At last, the rhythm of the drum slowed. The dancers' wings dropped. Their bodies bent forward. The wings dragged along the ground making a rustling noise that could be heard between drum beats. One by one, they spun away from the circle into the crowd of onlookers. They were enveloped by men offering ponchos and bottles of *trago*—cane alcohol. While the ponchos were being wrapped around them, they drank long pulls from the bottles.

Don José ushered me inside a thatched-roof hut where his family and those of other co-op members joined a group from the village. A trago bottle was passed around. We spent the rest of our stay inside the hut drinking and sharing food prepared by local families. I felt physically and emotionally drained.

It was not until the long drive back to Sinincay that I had the opportunity to talk with Don José. I inquired as to whether any messages had been received from dead ancestors. "Of course," he answered. "Many messages. But only one for our little cooperative. Soon you will sign a big contract. Then we must work very hard to satisfy it. Very, very hard."

About two weeks after the Birdmen ceremony I was stopped on the street by a large, blond man. I had seen him before from a distance. Although he was well over six feet tall, he had always been accompanied by several Ecuadorians. I had assumed he was a native, born perhaps to European emigrants, and was surprised when he spoke to me in English laced with a decidedly non-Spanish accent. "You're the gringo who works with the brickmakers' co-op?" he asked.

I told him I was. We shook hands. "Congratulations," he said. "What you are doing is admirable."

He explained that he was a Lutheran missionary from Norway. A member of his congregation had told him about the co-op. He invited me to lunch at the Hotel Crespo. As we ate, he outlined plans for building a school that would offer an alternative to the traditional Catholic-oriented education. "Cuenca has a couple of pretty good schools." He winked. "But we think ours will provide a little something extra.

"It will also be very different architecturally. Each room will be in a separate octagonal-shaped building. The walls will be brick. Ours will be the only structure in Cuenca where the bricks actually show. We won't cover them with adobe. It will be a real showpiece!

"You know better than I that this creates a problem since all bricks produced within hundreds of miles of here are fired in crude ovens. Most of these bricks are unacceptable. They are weak, cracked, and unattractive. Okay when covered with adobe, but for what we have in mind, no. So you see my dilemma? Only those bricks produced nearest the firebox will be acceptable to us, only the hardest and reddest. We can use nothing but the best.

"My proposition to you is straightforward. We will buy all our bricks from your co-op—probably more than you sold the entire last year—and we will pay triple the normal price. In exchange you must guarantee to deliver only the very best to us. From each truck that comes in we will expect to accept just a portion. The rest you must take away. They are yours to do with as you please. We want no part of them. And you must work with our engineer to establish a delivery schedule. We have no room for stockpiling. Yet we cannot delay construction while waiting for you to deliver. Drunk brickmakers, heavy rains—all those problems will be yours.

"One more thing I should mention. My engineer's name is Gomez. You have heard of him? Good. Then you know he is the best in Cuenca. He constructs the biggest buildings in this city. He is highly skeptical of our plans and constantly reminds me that Cuenca is not Oslo or Madrid. However, he promises that if we are successful he will use your brickmakers for his other projects."

I walked away from the Hotel Crespo overwhelmed with conflicting emotions. I was ecstatic and I was scared. What the Norwegian had suggested was unheard of among Andean brickmakers: both the opportunities and the obstacles to meeting his terms. I went directly to the co-op's warehouse.

Looking back, I can say that the remainder of my time in Cuenca gave me an education in the miracles of faith. I stayed on for another year. Despite what seemed like insurmountable problems, the members of the Sinincay co-op rose to the occasion. The Lutheran school was constructed with co-op bricks and it was indeed a showpiece. Engineer Gomez was true to his word; he contracted with us to supply bricks for a ten-story building, the largest in Cuenca. Don José took over my role. Although he was not invited into buena gente social circles, by the time I left he was treated as an equal in negotiating brick sales. He sat down with buena gente architects, engineers, and contractors. Together they worked out quality-control plans and schedules.

The miracle was not that the Birdmen had foretold the coming of the Norwegian Lutheran, nor that a contract had been signed. The miracle was that the Sinincay co-op members adjusted so quickly and successfully to the requirements imposed on them. They developed a schedule for producing and delivering bricks, for culling out only the best and setting the others aside for less-demanding buyers. These tasks had never before been performed by Quechua brickmakers—at least not in the memory of the oldest Sinincay resident. The members applied themselves to these and other aspects of their work with diligence and, except for a few minor errors, they succeeded. In essence, they changed their work ethic.

They revolutionized a system of doing business that had become ingrained over hundreds of years.

Don José did not mind talking about the ceremony of the Birdmen. He did not object to my questions about Tupa Inca and how the Birdmen related to the ancient priests. "They are all one and the same," he said simply enough. "What you saw is the same as what those warriors on the beach saw." However, he was reluctant to describe exactly what had happened. I always suspected he knew, that he himself had at one time or another participated as a member of the Birdmen. But he would neither confirm nor deny this.

One day as we sat on a pile of bricks in the warehouse yard soaking up the last rays of the afternoon sun, he confided as much as he ever would about the remarkable event.

"You tell me, Don José, that the Birdmen are exactly the same as Tupa Inca's priest," I said trying to goad him into an explanation, "yet that priest went somewhere. He flew across the ocean, or at least his soul or his spirit did. Upon returning, he was able to guide all those other warriors back to the island. Did the Birdmen also travel somewhere?

Don José pulled a dirty handkerchief from his pocket and mopped the sweat-soaked brick dust off his forehead. "Somewhere very far away. Like Tupa Inca's priest they flew a great distance."

"Where?"

"To the ancestors."

"And where are they?"

"Higher than the top of our tallest volcano. They reside near Mama Kilya. It is a long journey. Remember what Atahualpa said: The Quechua must always follow the ancestors' commands. Viracocha spoke to the Birdmen through their ancestors. The brickmakers obeyed Atahualpa's demand. Despite the hardships, the changes required of them, they did what they were told to do."

He carefully folded the handkerchief and returned it to his pocket. "And you," he said, "what did you learn?"

"I'm not certain, Don José, but I know I witnessed psychonavigation. And it works."

My last year with the brickmakers passed quickly. About two months into it I met a man from a Boston-based consulting firm. While working on an Ecuadorian hydroelectric project, he had visited Cuenca several times. Our first meeting was by chance, but afterwards he always invited me to dinner when he was in town. He was intrigued by my stories of the Shuara and the Birdmen.

During his final trip to Cuenca, he offered me a job. "We need a person with your skills," he said. "Most of all we need someone we can send to remote places without worrying about him cracking up." He gave me a long, serious look. "Come work for me when your tour with the Peace Corps ends, and I promise you'll see psychonavigation. I'll send you to Indonesia. If you think you've learned things here in Ecuador, wait 'til you get to Sulawesi!"

"Sulawesi?"

"The big island up near Borneo where the Bugis live."

I had never heard of the Bugis and told him so.

"The Bugis. Bogeymen! You know, those jeweled and turbaned pirates who scared hell out of European sailors a couple of hundred years ago. That's truly where we get the name—Bogeymen."

"They still exist?"

"Not only do they exist, they still sail pirate ships, wear pearls in their ears, turbans on their heads, and cutlasses in their sashes."

"You're kidding."

"I most certainly am not. I'm sure they still psychonavigate. Their ships have no instruments at all, not even compasses. Come and see for yourself. If you join us I promise you'll go to Indonesia—Java, Bali, and Borneo. New worlds for you. New experiences. Besides, you'll have access to the best minds at the United Nations, Asian Development Bank, and universities like the one in Canberra, Australia, where they specialize in such subjects."

It all seemed too easy. While my Peace Corps friends fretted about finding jobs back in the states, I fantasized about the places where this job could take me.

Three months before my scheduled departure, I told Don José about the job. He was as excited as I was.

"It's what you must do," he said. "We here, we Quechua, opened a door and you peeked in. What the Birdmen practice has been done forever. Everywhere. I know that as well as I know the trail from my house to the road. You may never become a Birdman, but you will learn to psychonavigate. Not here, not from us. You are not ready yet. Yes, go to Indonesia. Explore. Study. Visit as many places as you can!"

Whenever there is a difficult job to be done, I remember my Quechua education. I think of the Sinincay brickmakers, the obstacles they had to overcome, and the faith and determination that enabled them to succeed. I often hear people complain that to reverse our modern society's course of environmental destruction will require impossibly difficult changes in lifestyles and cultural patterns. Psycho-navigation has much to teach us in this regard—about ourselves, our environment, and our inner resources. It is a technique, available to each and every one of us, that can help us find our way even through a maze of the most difficult circumstances.

5

The Bugis: Soul-Wandering among Pirates

My boss was true to his word. Shortly after signing me up with his Boston firm, he sent me to the island of Java, on my first assignment as a bona fide management consultant. Our client, the Asian Development Bank, had a project manager who suggested I stop off at the University in Canberra, Australia. There I could meet with experts on various aspects of Indonesian culture and business. Several of them were familiar with psychonavigation, although none had tried it personally.

"I don't think it works for us," one professor told me. "We're too far removed from nature. To psychonavigate, you have to feel a special kinship with the environment—impossible for people who isolate themselves in skyscrapers, huge houses, and cars."

"But maybe if we learned to psychonavigate we would become less destructive," I suggested. "Maybe it could help us save the environment." I was painfully aware that I myself had not yet tried it.

The more I learned about psychonavigation, the stronger became my suspicions that technologically advanced societies are missing out on something special. It is easy for people from our culture, myself included, to find reasons why we should not or cannot do it. But such rationalizations are based on a view of the world that grows out of an industrialized approach to life, a belief that nature is an obstacle to be overcome, a force to be dominated. This assumption, that the concept of scarcity does not apply to the environment is totally erroneous and is foreign to the philosophies of psychonavigators.

Psychonavigating societies place a great emphasis on the harmony of the whole. Materialistic advancement is not an important goal for them. In fact, the key to psychonavigation seems to be a state of mind that includes a positive attitude and a belief in one's spiritual kinship with one's surroundings.

It was during that first trip to Indonesia that I met Toyup. He lived in the mountains near Bandung, West Java. Although he could not recall his age, his memories of working for the Dutch, and then for the Japanese after their invasion in World War II, were particularly vivid. When I knew him he must have been close to eighty. He was living proof that a person can travel great distances without changing his geographic location. It was Toyup who taught me that the true journey is the journey within.

Toyup showed me his technique for entering a mental framework known in the West as the alpha state. His personal story and his approach to dealing with problems contributed significantly to my first book, *The Stress-Free Habit* (Healing Arts Press, 1989). Although Toyup was not familiar with the word, when I described psycho-navigation to him, it was clear that he understood it completely. He was fascinated by the story of the Birdmen.

"We have people like that in Java," he told me, "and in Bali and Borneo."

I asked him to take me to a ceremony where I could meet such people. In his customary straightforward manner, he declined, saying it was more important for me to work at improving my own techniques.

"Your time will come," he said with a grin, but first he set about helping me to improve my Bahasa Indonesia, the official language of his country.

Toyup's assessment was correct. What I learned from him about the alpha state later became an important part of my own psycho-navigating experiences. A working knowledge of Bahasa Indonesia turned out to be a real asset. The hours I passed with Toyup contributed to my personal development in ways that enhanced my abilities to absorb and communicate to others the events I experienced in coming years.

Actual contact with Indonesian psychonavigation had to wait for a later trip. It did not take place anywhere near Toyup's beloved mountains. Instead, it occurred on one of the remote outer islands, far away from Java.

When my boss informed me that my second assignment would be

for three months in Sulawesi, I felt ecstatic. Perhaps I would get to meet the fabled Bugis.

I flew from Boston to Jakarta, Indonesia's capital city on the island of Java. My job required several days of meetings there before departing for Ujung Pandang, Sulawesi. After checking into the luxurious Hotel Indonesia, I called a friend from my former trip, a Javanese who worked for the Ministry of Economic Development.

We talked at length. Indonesian etiquette dictates an extended period of polite conversation before getting to the real point. Finally I felt my obligation had been fulfilled. I asked the question that had haunted my thoughts ever since the day my boss had given me this assignment.

"What do you know about the Bugis?"

"The Bugis? Oh yes, my friend. Of course. You are going to Sulawesi, land of the terrible Bugis! You've heard stories. You certainly will see plenty there. Come to my house for dinner and we'll talk. Okay?"

That evening, I found my Indonesian dinner host eager to discuss the Bugis tribe.

"They live mostly in Sulawesi. During olden times, they terrified your ancestors. European spice traders feared them as the fiercest, most blood-thirsty pirates in the world. Of course, the Bugis saw themselves differently. They were simply defending their lands; they manned our first line of defense against marauding sailors.

"Their tradition continues. Mostly, they ferry goods between the islands comprising our nation. Indonesia has over thirteen thousand islands. It takes lots of cargo space to fill the needs of all those ports! But we all know the Bugis have not abandoned their ways, not completely. You will hear many tales about them and their magnificent schooners, called prahus. Some of the stories are false, many true. Until very recently, their prahus carried no compasses, charts, or radar. A few still don't."

I was quite literally sitting on the edge of my seat. "How do they navigate? You're talking about some of the world's most treacherous waters. And extremely long voyages."

"Yes, I know. To survive all these centuries, the Bugis had to develop exceptional skills. They borrowed from many other traditions and learned to dream their way to destinations."

"Psychonavigation!"

"What's that?"

"We use the word 'psychonavigation' to describe this type of skill."

"I see. I am not familiar with that word."

"Similar skills are practiced by different people throughout the world. I didn't realize anyone still used it to navigate on water, though."

"A few Bugis do. But it's dying out, replaced by modern equipment. The Bugis, it is said, also design and build their prahus in trance. I have heard that their shipwrights become possessed by forest spirits and float into the woods to select the finest trees, resins, and other materials. According to tradition, they use only natural substances in their prahus—no metal, plastic, or anything man-made. They worship nature. You will see."

Ujung Pandang appeared on the horizon beneath and ahead of the DC-3 that was flying me to my next assignment. In former times this outpost city was called Makassar. It was located on one of the spice islands—later known as Celebes—sought by Columbus when he accidentally arrived in America. In an attempt to expunge all words reminiscent of the Colonial period, the government had recently renamed the island Sulawesi.

The plane began its descent. Slowly we circled above Ujung Pandang's harbor. For miles around all I could see was the vast, empty beach and the Java sea dotted with dozens of tiny atolls. The only sign of humanity was a small ancient city that seemed to cling to the very edge of a land shrouded in mystery. The interior of Sulawesi was a mass of rugged mountains. I had read that much of the island was unexplored except by tribes like the Toraja who claimed to have descended from another galaxy in "star ships."

As we descended, I could pick out the old stone fortress built more than three hundred years ago by Europeans intent on defending the spice trade. Dutch, Portuguese, and Spanish adventurers all sought their fortunes in Celebes; many died, a few grew rich.

Anchored off the crumbling ramparts were several large schooners. Buganese prahus! When I spied them lying quietly in the sapphire waters, my heart skipped a beat. My Javanese friend had told me that these magnificent sailing ships ply their trade from Cambodia and Singapore in the north, across the South China Sea, Malacca Strait, Java, Flores, and Banda Seas, all the way to New Guinea and Australia in the south; and from the Philippines in the east over the entire expanse of the Indian Ocean to Africa in the west. They are splendid vessels, a marriage of traditional island boats and seventeenth century Portuguese galleons. He had said that they comprise the only remaining fleet of cargo-hauling tall ships in the world. Now I looked down on them in their home port, on the island the Bugis call home.

The plane touched ground, and I thought of the work ahead in Sulawesi. The Bugis and their prahus would have to wait for now.

After deplaning at the Ujung Pandang airport, I was greeted by a man who introduced himself simply as Yosuf. He was short and wiry; his thick black hair swept away from his brow in curly waves. He wore a brown safari shirt, tan slacks, and leather sandals. His face was leathery with deep lines radiating from the corners of his mouth and eyes. Eventually I learned that he was less than forty years old and concluded that these lines were due to his habit of smiling nearly all the time, and of almost never being without a lighted clove cigarette. During my trips to Indonesia, I became accustomed to their fragrance. Even now, I associate the smell of cloves with Sulawesi and, especially, the Bugis.

Yosuf explained that he was one of several local people assigned to work with me and the other foreign consultants who had been retained by the Indonesian government to complete a study of Sulawesi's development potentials.

"You my master," he said in broken English as he drove me to the hotel. "I do as you command."

"Master!" That and the idea of commanding had ominous implications. "No. No, Yosuf. Perhaps you're my guide. Or host. Or. . . ."

"Ah, yes. I see clear." He turned his Toyota jeep into a cluster of bicycle-cabs at what seemed like a murderous speed. "You no like the word *master*." He laid on his horn. The bicycle drivers were unfazed. They ignored our jeep. Their cabs, like those throughout Indonesia, were decorated with fanciful scenes in bright pastel colors; passengers reclined in box-like seats in front of the peddling drivers. "I forget. In Indonesia, *master* is for teacher. I expect learn lots from you."

I decided to drop it at that. Perhaps, by remaining silent, I could encourage him to concentrate on the road and the bicycle cabs.

We pulled up in front of what once must have been a splendid Dutch colonial hotel. It was badly in need of paint. Through the open windows of the jeep I could smell rotting garbage.

"This is my hotel?"

"Ujung Pandang's best. Look. You view ocean." The sight of a magnificent prahu sailing past, not more than two hundred yards away, raised my spirits. "This truly the best." He winked. "Where Ujung Pandang leaders bring womans. Oh!" He rolled his eyes for emphasis. "Beautiful womans. Yes. Not wives, but other womans!"

A group of ragged boys lounged on the steps of the old hotel. He ordered several to take my luggage, then led me through the lobby, right past the reception desk, and up the stairs. On the second floor, we walked down a corridor that doubled as an inner balcony. Peering through the handrail to my left I glimpsed an unroofed garden courtyard. On our right were the doors to the hotel rooms. At number 208 he stopped. With a flourish, he produced a key from his pocket and opened the door.

The interior was like a cave. Yosuf trotted across the room and opened the wooden shutters with a clatter. "Oh, see." He motioned toward the harbor and a prahu as it glided toward the open ocean. Recalling the conversation at that dinner in Jakarta, I wondered whether this boat was piloted or had been designed by a psychonavigator.

The room itself was spacious enough. It contained a desk, two chairs, a closet, bathroom, and two large mahogany cabinets.

"But where is my bed?" I asked.

Yosuf looked very amused. "Obvious you no Dutch spy," he said as he shoved back a panel on one of the cabinets. Inside was a bed.

In my childhood, Hans Christian Anderson stories had taught me about Dutch beds; they had sounded warm and cozy, but I never was entirely comfortable in this one. I always felt as if I were crawling into a coffin. The army of lice I shared it with dispelled any romantic notions that might otherwise have lingered.

The best thing about the hotel was the splendid view of the harbor and the Buganese prahus. Every morning, as I opened the shutters, I was treated to a spectacle; the scene must have looked exactly as it had when Dutch East India Company ships plied these waters. I felt privileged to enjoy sights that had vanished from most of the world during the last century, but staying in this hotel with its lax approach to sewage disposal and sanitation exacted a toll. I dined in the hotel's restaurant on my first night there, and spent the next two days recovering from the ill-effects of the meal. Eventually Yosuf helped me move into a government guest house on the outskirts of town. I no longer enjoyed a view of the prahus; but the meticulous Javanese cook and her spotless kitchen were more than adequate compensation.

At the end of my second week, Yosuf suggested we spend Sunday together on one of the small atolls I had seen from the airplane. The motor launch departed early in the morning. At a U.S. resort its capacity would have been limited to perhaps twenty people. I counted sixty-five. It was about thirty feet long, wooden, with a small cabin at the bow where passengers stowed their belongings: baskets, towels, blankets, rattan and canvas bags. The launch was powered by a single outboard motor. Although the motor lacked any sort of identification, I judged it to be around 40 horsepower, manufactured during World War II or shortly thereafter. Fortunately, the Makassar Strait was unusually calm. The trip took slightly more than an hour. The passengers seemed happy to have a foreigner aboard, and provided me with many opportunities to bone up on my Bahasa Indonesia. Although different islands and tribes have their own dialects, the majority of Indonesians are able to speak this common language; it is used extensively in commerce and schools. Yosuf and the other Indonesians assigned to the consultants insisted that, while working, we all speak English, so I had not found many chances to practice the language Toyup had helped me learn.

The people on our launch shared food with each other. They joked and laughed a great deal. One small group broke into songs described by Yosuf as Celebes folk music. By the time we reached the dock at the atoll we all were singing together, even the foreigner who had absolutely no knowledge of the Celebes language and cannot carry the tune of even his favorite American songs.

The atoll was as beautiful as Yosuf had promised. No larger than a baseball park, it was heavily vegetated with coconut palms and tropical flowers. Trails wound around the central hill and up to the lookout at the top; from here the view of Ugung Pandang in the distance, the prahus, and other boats entering and exiting the harbor was spectacular. Despite the several hundred people visiting on this particular Sunday, most of the island was uncrowded. The visitors congregated at the north end where a long wooden pier had been built out over the emerald waters. Since the atoll was surrounded by a jagged coral reef, serious swimmers and divers were well advised to take advantage of the pier. They could walk to the end, dive off into the deep water beyond the reef, and swim back to the pier's ladder. Some wore goggles; after borrowing a set, I understood why. The reef, a rainbow of colors, was inhabited by millions of tropical fish.

"Be careful of great white sharks," Yosuf shouted to me from the pier. He threw back his head and laughed.

I laughed too. But after that I kept looking over my shoulders and stuck close to the pier. It occurred to me that the movie about great whites, *Blue Water, White Death*, had been filmed north of Australia, perhaps not very far from Sulawesi.

Where the pier joined the land there was a well-worn path leading to a refreshment stand. Shortly before noon, Yosuf suggested we go there to buy soft drinks and coconuts.

We took our purchases and the basket of sandwiches Yosuf had brought from the guest house to a secluded area at the opposite end of the island. Here there were no other visitors, just coral outcroppings, scrub palms, and solitude.

"You like?"

"Very much. How come no one else is here?"

"Sulawesi peoples together peoples. Like crowds, okay? But I know American peoples alone peoples time to time. I think you like this place."

"Well, Yosuf, you're right. This is like being in paradise."

When we finished our lunch, I asked if it would be all right for me to take a swim.

"Okay, but very bad," he said. "Coral sharp and go out far. See. Where water turn black, there end." I followed his finger and could see that, perhaps 200 feet out, the color of the water changed from emerald to dark purple. The reef extended that far. Beyond, there was only the Java Sea. Except for a single black cloud peeking over the horizon, the sky was azure.

"I could wear my tennis shoes."

"Yes. You do that you be okay. But no fall."

I laced on my tennis shoes and stepped in. Immediately I felt the jagged bottom as it stabbed into my feet. It was much rougher than I had expected: a solid mass of unyielding coral. The water came up just above my ankles. I moved forward, stumbled, and caught my balance. For a moment I envisioned myself tripping, twisting an ankle, and falling onto the sharp outcroppings. The thought nearly convinced me to turn back until I realized how much face I would lose by doing so.

It was slow work and I had to concentrate. I forced myself to be patient and very meticulous as I continued toward the shelf's edge. But there were also compensations. The water was cool, a pleasant contrast to the heat of the sun. The coral beneath the clear surface shimmered in incandescent colors. When I stopped to look back, I was treated to a view of the atoll, which at this end was so idyllic that I could imagine it was Robinson Crusoe, instead of Yosuf, sitting on the shore. He appeared to be lost in meditation. A light breeze stirred the palms behind him. Occasionally the silence was broken by the loud screech of a parrot.

As the water grew deeper, walking became easier. In addition, my feet developed a certain sensitivity to the coral, allowing me to relax my concentration. I became engrossed in the shimmering water and the brilliant colors of the coral beneath. My attention was focused on the world under my feet. I had become a part of that world and had lost all sense of time.

I felt a sudden coolness on my face and shivered from the chill. Around me, the water lost its sparkle; it turned dark. I stopped and looked out to sea. The deeper water was choppy. Above, a huge ominous cloud covered the sun. Coming from the horizon, it had nearly gained our atoll. When I realized that the water was almost up to my chest I knew that I was far from shore. Looking again to the sea, I witnessed an explosion of water as a school of fish burst into the air along the edge of the shelf. I was no more than fifteen feet away from the shelf. An involuntary shudder rippled along my spine. I glanced back at the atoll. Yosuf looked very distant. I peered at him, and suddenly it dawned on me that he was standing in the shallow water, waving his arms frantically.

I sensed the danger before I saw it. Perhaps the leaping fish had stirred my subconscious. Turning to the Java Sea I somehow knew what I would find.

His eye was huge. Unblinking, it stared right into mine. The dorsal fin arched high above the water. It hesitated, then disappeared. A giant tail slapped the water before submerging. I froze. The great white must have been as long as the distance between me and the edge of the coral shelf where he hunted; perhaps three times my own height! I was seized by an almost irrepressible urge to run. Yet something, an inner voice, told me to stand still. He won't leave the deep trench, the voice said—unless you do something stupid. Stay put.

I stared into the black water. How far did the shelf fall away? I could see nothing and could only wonder whether he had dived into the abyss or was stealing across my reef. Time went by slowly. I counted to one hundred. Then I knew I would not see him again, except perhaps later in my nightmares. Slowly I made my way back to shallow water and then dashed for shore, the dangers of the jagged coral suddenly forgotten. Yosuf was waiting under a palm. For the first time, I realized it was raining. A streak of lightning lit up the sky, followed by a resounding clap of thunder.

"Good you get out," Yosuf said. "Water very bad in 'lectric storm!"

"Didn't you see him Yosuf?"

"See who?"

"The great white!"

"Great white? No. I see no shark. Where?"

"Right beside me. On the reef's edge. There." I pointed.

"Too far for me to see. But," he laughed, "no surprise. They all around this area. Kill many relatives."

"Relatives?"

"Yes. My grandfather and uncle both die from shark. Many Bugis go that way."

"Yosuf!" I was astounded that the thought had not occurred to me before. "You're a Bugi?"

"Of course—well, mostly anyway."

July fourth came several days after our visit to the atoll. I had hoped to spend it with Yosuf. Ever since I had learned of his heritage, I had difficulty concentrating on my work. I was eager to hear more about Buganese culture, especially prahu building and navigation. However, Indonesians do not celebrate the U.S. Independence Day, and Yosuf and the rest of the Indonesian staff were required to report for work.

Charlie, the administrative manager of the U.S. team and the most senior member, was a sailing buff. He too was fascinated with prahus. When he learned that I had a 16-mm movie camera, he arranged to rent a small motor boat with a pilot.

"I'll pay for the ride," he said, "if you promise to send me a copy of the film when we get back to the States."

The Fourth of July was a gorgeous day, perfect for filming the harbor. The only problem was our surly and uncooperative pilot. He pretended not to understand Bahasa Indonesia, and spoke only a few English phrases. We spent two hours with him as he chugged around the wharfs. Charlie finally insisted that he take us outside the harbor.

"We want to see Bugi prahus under sail," Charlie explained. "We want pictures." He pointed to my camera and held up his hands pantomiming the filming of a movie.

"Bugis, sure," replied the pilot. He gunned the engine, nearly spilling Charlie overboard. Fifteen minutes later, we approached one of the giant catamaran rafts used in this part of the world for fishing. When not under sail, and from a distance, they look like platforms built on stilts rising from the ocean. But in the water, when the sails are hoisted, they move remarkably fast. The raft itself rises high above the pontoons, and can be as large as a single family house in a middle class American suburb. It is strewn with nets, lines, sails, and usually includes a small home where the fishermen and their families live.

"That's not a prahu," Charlie complained to the driver.

"Yes, Bugis." He held up his hand as if he were filming, in imitation of Charlie's earlier pantomime. "Here, yes, Bugis."

The people on the raft were very friendly. They invited us aboard; and not only encouraged my filming, but greatly added to it by staging several scenes: dropping anchor, lowering and hauling nets, hoisting sails, and cooking a meal—all while speeding through the water. When we departed, we presented them with a bag containing the candy bars, peanut butter, and crackers we had brought along for sustenance. This pleased them, although it was, I am certain, small compensation for their disappointment at learning that my film could not be developed until after I returned to the United States.

By the time we left, it was late afternoon. We had seen prahus tied up to docks, or sailing in the distance; but had not gotten close to one under sail. Although the day had been enjoyable, and I ended up with some memorable film footage, we were nevertheless rather frustrated.

When I told our story to Yosuf the next day, he listened attentively. He asked me to describe the boat we had rented and its pilot. Then, atypically, he frowned.

"Him bad man. I know. Kill prahu captain. Knife fight. No long ago. Now stay away from prahus." Then his face lighted. "You want see prahus? Why no tell Yosuf? I show you prahus. Plenty. Sure. The real thing. Very special prahus. Yes."

On our next free day Yosuf and I left early. We drove for nearly two hours along a double-lane paved road. Eventually it narrowed and turned to dirt. Then it became barely more than a trail through tall palms. Glimpses of the sea appeared off to our left. Every now and then I caught sight of a white sandy beach. Yosuf chattered constantly. Uncharacteristically, he sometimes mixed *Bahasa* in with his English. He was obviously more excited than usual.

"I live very close here 'til sixteen. Take many, many sailings from this place. All over Indonesia." He laughed. "Loved many beautiful womans."

He jerked the wheel and the jeep turned sharply to the left. The wheels spun in the sand and then we shot through a clump of low bushes. Suddenly my heart was in my throat. I could not believe the sight in front of us.

There at the end of the road was a huge prahu. It was high and dry, perhaps fifty feet from the water's edge, propped upright by rows of stakes that resembled roots sprouting from its hull into the sandy beach. It was new—brand, spanking new—an unlaunched virgin. To me it looked like a picture of Noah's ark under construction I had cherished as a child. Around it were a dozen or more men laboring diligently. Some were busy with the hull itself, others worked in little groups or individually off to the side, with adzes, hatchets, and hand drills, preparing pieces for later use.

"Oh. Beautiful!" exclaimed Yosuf. "Okay, we go forward?"

"Yes, indeed." I felt I was seeing something I had waited all my life for. Images of Long John Silver and Francis Drake filled my mind.

He drove a hundred feet closer before shutting off the engine. I had not taken my eyes off the prahu. Now that we were near it, I was amazed to see hundreds of wooden sticks protruding like porcupine quills from its hull. "What are those, Yosuf?"

"Bugis no use nails. This prahu has no metal. Just wood. Those hold boat together." They were wooden pegs.

"They expand in water?" I held my hands together and then moved them apart. "Swell?"

"Yes. Yes. Better than nails. See?" He pointed at a man perched high on a platform, who was pounding a peg deeper into the hull with a wooden mallet. "All wood is blessit by forest—" he searched for a word. "You know." He made a face, sticking out his tongue and waving his hands around his ears.

"Blessed by forest spirits?" I was astonished by what I was saying.

"Yes. Yes. Blessit by spirits. Everything on prahu comes from forest: bamboo, rattan, coconut shell, sweet palm. All blessit by spirits. If boat maker forget, if one log not blessit, bad spirit come sneak in— boat sink. Many mans die. Come."

We left the jeep and walked up to a spot directly under the bow. The wood smelled wonderfully fresh. Its fragrance blended with that of the sea. Yosuf exchanged greetings with several of the workers. Three men who had been sitting by the stern stood and walked slowly toward us. Yosuf tugged my arm and we headed to meet them. He yelled a greeting in Bahasa Indonesia. Then to me, "The old one Buli. Bugis' best prahu maker. Others, students."

Buli was short and stooped. His hair was a mop of white. His weather-beaten skin suggested many years at sea under the hot equatorial sun. He had no front teeth. Although he never confided his age, he looked to be in his eighties. His students were young, perhaps in their early twenties. All three were dressed in traditional batik sarongs whose colors had been bleached by the sea and sun. Their short-sleeved white shirts were unbuttoned down the front. Like the other workers, they went barefoot. One of the students sported a black felt *peci* hat, a style favored by Muslims. Another's head was wrapped in a bright red scarf, trailing a long tail down his back. It reminded me of the pirate tales that are so much a part of Bugi legends. Watching them approach, I wondered whether there was any truth to the idea that they could design prahus by means of psychonavigation. Did they, as legend had it, actually levitate and float into the forests to select the materials they used? Of course, such thoughts were contrary to the beliefs I had been raised with, but I had learned in Ecuador that the world is not as cut-and-dried and rational as our scientists might like us to believe.

Buli greeted Yosuf with enthusiasm. In *Bahasa*, he assured me that a friend of Yosuf's was a friend of his. He patted my shoulder warmly. Later I would learn that this was an unusual gesture, especially since I was a person of European descent. He led us back to the place near the stern where he had been seated, sending his students off for hot tea and rice cakes.

While we waited for the students to return, Buli and Yosuf talked about their families and work. Whenever we were with other Bugis, Yosuf spoke *Bahasa*, a language we all understood. It seemed to me that Buli was merciless as he teased Yosuf for forsaking the traditional Buganese life in favor of government work in the city. Yosuf made no attempt to defend himself; he simply laughed along with the older man.

Finally the tea and cakes arrived. Yosuf briefed the three men on my background and explained about my interest in the prahus; he emphasized that I was truly sympathetic to Bugi ways and was not like any other European or American he had met. This seemed to make a profound impression upon our hosts, and for this I was extremely grateful. They bowed to me. After that they seemed to accept me, if not as one of them, then at least as a welcome guest.

Yosuf then told me that Buli had started building prahus at an early age, as a student under his grandfather, a famous shipwright who was killed by the Japanese during their invasion of Indonesia in World War II. His family's fame reached far. In 1962 Buli was recruited by a Taiwanese boat company to help them build sailing yachts. He had spent several years in Taiwan, but had found it frustrating.

"They build boats without love or regard for nature," Buli told me, speaking very slowly and precisely in *Bahasa*. "Everything is metal or plastic except the hull. When I was there, they wanted me to design boats made of fiberglass. A standard boat," he spat. "To me that is devil worship. They use molds. All their boats are alike. Bah. Who wants that?" He pointed at his prahu. "Each of my boats is a living spirit like you and me. Each is different. Each must come from nature. Everything on my prahus is natural. Everything."

After we finished our meal, Buli took his students aside for a long talk, apparently instructing them in tasks requiring their attention. Then he gave Yosuf and me a tour of the boat he was building, and of another that was laid up for repairs in the shallows farther down the beach. His claim about natural materials was no exaggeration. Even the seams of the teak decks were caulked with a sticky palm fiber. The ropes were woven from coconut husks. Wooden blocks were fastened into place with strips of rattan. Masts and booms were sculpted from jungle trees. There was no electronic or navigational equipment on either prahu, not even a compass.

"I have heard that your captains are able to navigate without instruments," I ventured. "How do they accomplish this?"

"I think you already know the answer," he said with a twinkle. "They do it the same way that I design prahus."

His answer nearly took my breath away, but I tried not to let it show. "I have heard this, yes. That it is done through dreaming, while in a trance."

"You might describe it so."

"But I have heard many stories. Some say that while in this state, you rise up and fly through the forests to select the best woods."

Buli laughed. "You find such a thing difficult to believe?"

"In my culture we do not do it."

"No. You build prahus of metal and fiberglass. Molds."

"Then it is true what they say?"

"You are a perceptive person. You ask me a serious question, and deserve a serious answer. I need more time with you to give you a true answer." He turned to Yosuf, "You will arrange another visit?" Turning back to me, he bowed.

I placed my fingertips together and returned his bow. "Thank you. I look forward to our next visit."

During the drive back to Ujung Pandang, I worked at convincing myself that visits with the shipwright were justifiable as part of my job. Yosuf, who did not share my need for rationalizations, listened patiently. "After all," I said, "much of this island's commerce relies on prahus. Shipbuilding is an important component of the local economy. Don't you agree?"

"Yes, agree." He hit the horn: two short blasts down an empty road. "We return soon!"

Our second visit contrasted sharply with the first. Yosuf pulled the jeep up beside the virgin prahu. Everything looked much the same as before, except there was not a soul anywhere in sight.

"Is today a holiday?" I asked. Then I noticed the anxiety in Yosuf's face. He got out and inspected the work completed on the hull. He turned and briskly walked to the stern. Following at a respectful distance, I saw him stop, peer down the beach, and disappear behind the prahu. I ran after him. When I reached the stern, I nearly crashed into his back. He grinned at me, pointed, and broke into a chuckle.

"They launch oldie," he said in English, indicating with his outstretched arm the prahu that had been beached for repairs. It was aswarm with Buli's workers.

As luck would have it, we had picked a bad day for visiting the shipwright. While launching the old prahu, he had discovered a defect in one of the two long rudders used for steerage and stability. We watched for nearly three hours as the Bugis struggled to prop it back up on the stakes. At one point, the boat nearly toppled into the sea. After finally managing to get it under control, the workers spent the remainder of the day frantically repairing the rudder. Although what we saw was interesting, there was no opportunity for a relaxed discussion about psychonavigation.

Two weeks later, Yosuf announced it was time to try again. He assured me that things would be quiet. He had learned from a friend that the rudder had been repaired, and the prahu sailed once more. Our Javanese cook had packed a lunch in brightly colored baskets, and we headed out. We arrived at mid-day.

Yosuf's information proved correct. The old prahu was gone. The new one, still resting in its cradle of root-like stakes, was much more advanced than it had been during our first and second visits. It had been painted white. In fact, it looked so complete that I feared we might get caught up in another launching.

"Not for many weeks," Yosuf said, speaking *Bahasa* as was his custom among the Bugi. "The shell is good, yes, but that is only the outside. There is much more to do. The inside must be completed," his expression was unusually stern, "and the spirit of the prahu."

Buli was delighted to see us. After the customary exchange of news, he apologized for the confusion on our previous visit. His students were nowhere in sight. This, he said with a laugh, was because they were working inside the hull of the new prahu. "It is hotter than a volcano there, but that is very, very good for young men. Lots of sweat, lots of knowledge!"

He led us to a clump of trees near the edge of the sea. An assistant appeared and spread out a batik with an intricate design depicting a battle between mythical heroes. Yosuf opened the baskets and distributed our lunch. When the assistant returned with hot tea, he was rewarded by an invitation from Buli to join us.

"Enough food here to feed a full crew on the high seas," the shipwright said. "What we don't eat will go to the men." He waved his arms toward the prahu.

"Do the sailors eat well on a voyage?" I asked.

"Very well for a few days." Buli's laughter was echoed by Yosuf and the assistant. "If the trip lasts longer," he shrugged, "who knows? Everything depends on what the sea offers."

"One time," Yosuf volunteered, "a prahu I was aboard became becalmed for many days. All our food eaten. We dove overboard and picked barnacles off the hull. An excellent stew!"

I looked dubiously at the food in front of me. "I guess we're all different," I said. Everyone laughed.

"Yes," Buli said. He held his hands in front of his face, palms out. Slowly he brought them together. The two thumbs and two pointer fingers touched. He moved his hands around so that the palms faced me. His eyes looked at mine—serious now, any sign of mirth gone—through the space framed by his thumbs and fingers, a space shaped roughly like a diamond. "People are different," he said holding his hands motionless. "Each sees the world according to his own ideas. Who is to say what is correct? Is it not a matter of how we look? What we choose to see?"

"I agree with what you say." I sensed that something important had passed between us.

"My ancestors were heroes, yet to your ancestors they were devils." He lowered his hands.

"You know about 'Bogeymen' then?"

He bowed, "And yet, despite the differences between people, certain things have always been understood. Everyone, except for a very few, shares them. You are curious about how our captains navigate prahus."

"Yes, and how you design them."

"Of course. It is the same." He spread his hands over the batik cloth before us like a gambler fanning a deck of cards. "See this picture? It symbolizes the two selves. Down here at the bottom are two opposing armies led by two famous generals. These represent the everyday, physical world. Up here at the top are the spirit selves of the generals. See? These are able to wander into higher realms to receive guidance and return with this guidance to the physical selves. The physical selves are then free to turn this knowledge into action."

Buli's description reminded me of the Shuara shaman whose soul wandered off to join the jaguar and then returned to lead the warriors to the animal. "That is the way your captains navigate?" I asked.

"It is the old way. The right way. Known as the 'two selves' approach. It is not unique to us Bugis. Many, many people throughout time have used it. You see, one self—the spirit, if you like—leaves the body and takes a long voyage, 'the voyage to truth.' Not always does it see the real path. But if the selves have been dutiful to the gods and are endowed with the correct qualities, the true vision will appear, and the spirit self will be led down the real path. Then it can return and show the way to the other part of the self."

"Do you actually fly?" I knew of no word to express the idea of levitation.

"Fly? But of course we do. That is to say, the spirit self does. How else could our captains use this method to find their way across vast oceans? How could ship makers, like me, find the perfect tree amidst all the trees in the forest? The 'two selves' approach brings bliss to the person using it and is, as Europeans say, 'efficient,'" he sighed. "Unfortunately, although it is the right way, it is dying out among my people. Many have grown lazy. They have lost this ability, and now rely on metal and glass gadgets. You must be skilled to practice the two selves approach. It requires much training, patience, and years of application. The new generation lacks the necessary fortitude."

"No discipline," Buli's assistant spat in disgust.

"This is all most interesting," I said. My heart was beating faster than normal, but I tried not to let my excitement show for fear of offending my host. "What sort of training is required? What qualities must a person have?"

Buli did not hesitate. "Two characteristics are essential: a belief in the power of nature and a positive attitude." He lifted his hands and outlined a circle enclosing his body. "Nature is supreme, all energy is generated by her. People need only accept what she offers. We must not misuse her, or insult her. That is why I place such importance on building my boats from natural materials. Nature is perfect. My only chance of attaining perfection occurs when nature and all the spirits watching over her are on my side. For her to be with me, I must accept what she offers and use it wisely."

"I have heard similar philosophies expressed by others in distant parts of the world who also practice what you call the two selves approach."

"Wise people," said Yosuf.

"I wish more people in my own country believed it."

Buli spoke softly to me. "Perhaps it is your destiny to help them. You must try. But remember one other thing. We can accomplish nothing unless we believe in what we do. To design a worthy prahu, you must have faith. You have to think positively. No one can use the 'two selves approach' unless he believes it will work. For these generals to be victorious," he pointed to the ones in the top section of the batik, "they must think positively. The one who is most positive will be the most favored. His army will win."

"Can you move, like these generals, from one self to the other and back again?"

"Of course. I can and must in order to build prahus."

"How?"

"First I visualize. Well," he smiled, "of course, first—really first— I must clear my mind and visit the spirits."

"What does that mean?"

"Meditate. I meditate and totally relax until my body is as dead. Everything seems to stop: my brain, my heart, my stomach and lungs. I journey to the land of the spirits. They show me where the prahu I am about to build will go. What storms and reefs it will encounter. I see all this, visualizing it through the eyes of the spirits. They show me so I'll know where the prahu needs strength. Then later I call upon the spirits again to help me select the proper materials: wood for the hull and decking, trees that will be trimmed into masts. Everything."

My thoughts returned to Ecuador. The scene was as clear as day. "Sounds like the Birdmen," I said, without realizing I had spoken aloud.

The three exchanged glances. "Sometimes," said Buli, "our captains take the form of spirit birds. They fly out over the seas and return with knowledge of what lies beyond. This allows them to navigate safely."

"When I was eight years old," Yosuf said, "I was cabin boy on a prahu headed for Ceylon. My father was crew. Our captain prided himself on being modern; he used navigational equipment he had purchased in Jakarta. The Indian Ocean can become very angry in no time at all. We were hit by a terrible typhoon. I have never been so scared before or since. Our captain was killed when the main mast fell on him; he was washed overboard. After the storm had ended, we discovered that the box containing the sextant, compass, and chronometer was missing.

We were in the middle of the ocean, weeks from land and had no idea where we were, or what direction we should take. There was no one on board who knew anything about modern navigation. Then an old man named Rasmon stepped forward. He called us all together near the wheel. He told us that he would guide the boat to Ceylon. He instructed us to repair and re-step the mast. This took two days, but finally was completed, although the mast was shorter than before. The next morning, he assembled us again.

"He announced that during the night a bird had entered his body and transported his other self across the ocean to the coast of Ceylon. As he flew, he had taken careful note of the location of certain stars pointed out by the bird. Now, he said, he would employ those stars to guide us to our destination. It would take eight days and seven nights. Of course, every man there knew that this was the way all prahus had once been navigated. Someone asked Rasmon whether he had ever done this before. He looked from one to the other. 'Many times,' he said. I remember well his next words: 'Before most of you were born, before all the fancy equipment was born!' My father came up to me afterward. He told me that this would either be my last voyage or the most memorable.

"Every night Rasmon sat on the deck, meditating and contemplating the stars. Every morning he told the helmsmen where to steer. The days went by. On the eighth day, we all felt discouraged. My father spent most of that day in prayer. About noon a strong wind came up. Then shortly before sunset, a lookout perched high in the rigging called out the most wonderful two words I had ever heard in my young life, 'land ahead!' We were not far into the eighth night when we dropped anchor. Our prahu had reached Ceylon!"

Images of Ecuador and memories of another conversation returned. I briefly described Ecuador and gave a short history of the Incas. Then I told them the story of Tupa Inca and the more recent *Kon-Tiki* voyage. When I had finished, they all agreed that what Rasmon and other Bugis had done—whether in the form of birds or as other spirits—was similar to the feat accomplished by Tupa Inca's priest.

In the summer of 1989, I received a copy of an article entitled "Of Metaphysics and Polynesian Navigation." It had appeared in *Avaloka*, a journal of religious and cultural studies.* The author, James Barr, described himself as "a Seaman and a navigator." He stated:

> On several occasions in the early 1980's, I chose to study with four men who held the craft of open sea navigation. These venerable gentlemen were Tranhei Théki, (Maori), J. W. Kei (Tahiti), Jacques Koah (Bora Bora), and Matthew Burke Moi (Rorotonga and Western Samoa). My studies, excepting those with Théki, all took the form of discourse while at sea, for I served as a deck-hand and cook aboard their vessels. Before my service, I had no idea that the art of navigation (in the traditional sense) was still alive in Oceania. Still less did I know the nature of the traditional Polynesian world, and its similarity to other systems with which I was familiar.

Mr. Barr was fascinated by the fact that, although "Oceania is comprised of small islands and coral outcroppings, isolated by thousands of sea-miles," cultural similarities among the different peoples are strong.

> In fact, the cultural differences between the various islands are slight enough that the Polynesians can be said to hold a more or less unified world-view, with only minor variations. In order to explain such a

* See *Avaloka*, Vol. III: 1 and 2, pp 1–8.

unity, one must needs look to the method of transportation used to cross the watery abyss. One must seek out the navigators and their craft.

The navigational system described in his article is similar to that employed by the Bugis. He presents a three-step approach: the "literal" involving the everyday physical world; the "moral" or "subtle realm" above the literal that "draws one higher"; and the "anagogical" indicating an "absolute level," a transcendence like the higher soul in the Bugi's two-souls approach.

> The first level—the literal—entailed watching the clouds, the sea birds, the waves, and the colour of the sea. To accomplish this one must clear the mind of all excess thought and focus one's full attention upon phenomena as they arise. I was made to understand that years of practise were involved in this process. One must be taught to "look," to "see" the subtle aspects of change, and to apply these to the task of direction finding.

In order to proceed to the second and third steps, the practitioner must become relaxed, entering a state of meditation.

> In essence, one must fill one's lungs to capacity and concentrate all one's attention upon the act of breathing. This must be done while in a vessel far enough from land that one can feel the rising and falling of the swells. One attunes one's breath to the swells, so that as the vessel is lifted, one inhales deeply, "all the way to the feet," and as the vessel descends, one must exhale slowly with the swell. By this practise one's mind "becomes the sea," and one is able to commune directly with the element, so that any change is noticed at once. One must "commune with the body of the Lord of Waves," so as to know His mind as one's own.

The second step involves communication with a guide or an Inner Pilot, in this case a culturally shared entity.

> Tuaraati, the Ocean Lord, is addressed in a series of recited prayers, and a coconut is broken open, the juice of which is allowed to fall into the sea as a libation, while Tuaraati is asked to guide the mind of the navigator over his realm.

At this point, the practitioner enters the third stage: he realizes the route that he and his boat should follow.

> One must call the Lord of the Sea (Tuaraati) and listen to His in-

struction via His body, and then "know His mind." "Knowing" Tuaraati, one then is able to know the "Supreme One Tangaroa; He is the One who sails your canoe." One "knows" the sea, one "moves with it," and through Tangoroa via Tuaraati, one sails one's canoe to the destination.

The practitioner, like Rasmon in Yosuf's story, relies upon the stars to assist in this process. The stars act as guides to help what the Bugis refer to as the spirit self in its task of assisting the lower, physical soul.

Essentially, the stars are living entities which can be approached if one's mind is "filled with the sea," as discussed above. They must be approached via the Lord of Waves (Tuaraati) and "known" through Him. These beings are able to provide both direction (literal), and advice (moral), but they must be known or approached via the medium of the Lord of Waves, and hence Tangaroa (anagogical).

I was enthralled by this description of navigational techniques practiced by the Polynesians. Undoubtedly, the Bugis and the Polynesians have encountered each other many times over the centuries. Their traditional approaches to navigation have a great deal in common. Even more fascinating is the evidence that they both share so much with the jungle cultures of the Amazon, and with the Quechua high in the Andes, on the opposite side of the planet.

It would take another trip to Ecuador for me to begin to comprehend the magnitude of these interlocking relationships. Back in the country where it had all begun for me, I would finally be introduced to scientific explanations of how and why psychonavigation works.

6

Pichincha: Exploring a Theory

War had erupted in the Boston Headquarters while I was in Sulawesi. My company's mainline business was providing engineering services to industries, utilities, government agencies, and emerging high-tech establishments. About 80 percent of this work was in the United States. Many of the company owners, who were also its managers, defended the status quo. However, another group—one of growing influence—stressed the importance of international markets, emphasizing the need to diversify by expanding what they referred to as the "soft profitables," nonengineering disciplines with extremely high markups like management consulting.

My own future in the company was at stake. I was considered part of the "soft profitables." Political in-fighting was a new experience for me, and I had to admit that the idea of taking up a sword had its own appeal; I decided to jump into the fray.

I actively pursued consulting jobs in foreign countries, especially in Kuwait, Saudi Arabia, Iran, and other newly rich OPEC nations. The timing was right; I brought in a lot of work, and had to hire people to help complete it. Fortunately, a ready pool was available from the universities in the Boston area. For overseas assignments, I sought out former Peace Corps Volunteers.

Twenty-nine months after I returned from Sulawesi, the president retired. My side had won. There were thirty employees reporting to me. By company standards, it was a magic number, enough to call a department. More importantly, as a department manager, I was eligible to become an owner. Later that same year my name was thrown into the hat, and I was elected into the hallowed ranks of American capitalists by the Board of Directors.

The period of corporate warfare and the years that followed were a unique education. My classroom was one few business professors

69

will ever enter. The fact is I had created my job myself, although I probably would not have done so in a different political climate. Despite its obvious benefits, the job carried heavy burdens. I traveled frequently, but never stayed more than a week in any one place. The demands on my time did not give me the opportunity to meet people like Toyup or Buli, or to search out psychonavigational events.

Then, by chance, I met an amazing person.

His name was Julio Sinchi—a prominent Bolivian lawyer educated in philosophy and law at Harvard. I happened to sit next to him on a flight from Miami to a business conference in La Paz. At first, I saw him only in terms of what he could do for me; he was influential, and his friendship could help establish my company's presence in his country. Soon, however, I began to value this man for very different reasons.

During the week in La Paz, Julio and I spent several evenings together. We visited cafés frequented by writers, politicians, artists, and journalists. On the weekend, he took me to out-of-the-way museums, and we wandered around the open-air markets.

He loved to talk, and was a skilled listener. He had never been to Indonesia, but he was fascinated by my tales of the Javanese and the Bugis.

"I know well what you mean when you speak of the Bugis. Soul-wandering. Yes, we have our share of it here in Bolivia too. Psycho-navigation: A wonderful word, isn't it?" Then Julio surprised me. "Have you ever seen a *dalang*?"

As soon as he asked, I realized that he understood something profound about an event I had experienced, although I had never made the connection before. Nevertheless, the question came as a shock. "Dalang?" I asked in amazement.

"Yes. The Indonesian puppet master. I thought when you were in Java or Bali you might have come across one."

I had not thought about that night in Bandung for a long time. But once I began describing it, the scene returned quickly. It was a sidewalk theater, with dozens of people sitting in portable chairs or standing in the shadows behind. My Indonesian hosts kept me supplied with hot tea, little pastries, and *saté* (tiny bits of meat cooked in peanut oil over an open fire) purchased from all-night street vendors. The dalang worked alone. He had over a hundred shadow puppets and spoke for each in a different voice. He also played the *gamalong,* an instrument like the xylophone, with a sound resembling temple bells. He managed to play it all by himself, while simultaneously manipulating all the puppets! My hosts told me that the puppets spoke in four distinct languages. I could only understand one, Bahasa Indonesia, and that none too well. My hosts translated. The show combined traditional legends with current events. As I told Julio about that evening, I remembered aloud that the dalang predicted the death of a local politician who was struck down by a car within a month of the prediction—the papers suggested assassination.

"Interesting," said Julio thoughtfully. "I have heard this before, that they can foretell events. They are greatly respected, listened to by many of Indonesia's most famous leaders. True dalangs are highly trained and have completed years of apprenticeship. As you saw for yourself, they are master puppeteers. Many are brilliant musicians and accomplished linguists. Yours was one of these, yes? Imagine keeping all the languages and voices straight! Their powers of concentration are phenomenal; this requires discipline of mind and spirit as well as the body. To perform for so long, they must be able to draw on tremendous inner reserves. They have learned the ability to absorb energy from sources around the body and channel it for specific purposes. They are skilled in the arts of yoga and meditation. I am told that a good dalang becomes one with each puppet as soon as he takes that character's part. His soul merges with it. Never does he confuse the personalities or their roles."

My thoughts wandered to the jaguar-god of the Shuara. It seemed as though the puppets were a vehicle through which the dalang extended his consciousness to encompass otherwise "hidden" information. Like the jaguar-god, the puppets served as a link between the psychonavigator and his own inner knowledge—the knowledge that can "see" beyond time and space.

Julio's knowledge of other cultures and psychonavigation was more extensive than mine. Our discussions reawakened my desire to know more. Office politics in Boston had sidetracked me. Now I was once again able to appreciate the importance of acquaintances like Teofilo, Tanya, Don José, Toyup, Yosuf, and Buli. Julio brought yet another dimension to this field of discovery: Part Quechua, he was steeped in the traditions of the Bolivian Andes, but he also saw with the eye of a Western scholar. His Harvard education offered new perspectives on these ancient practices.

I was in La Paz for only six days. I had meetings to attend and Julio's law practice kept him very busy. When the day came for my return to Boston, he drove me to the airport. We promised we would meet again.

Several years later, I received a letter postmarked Quito, Ecuador. It was from Julio. Political unrest had forced him to leave Bolivia. He had moved to Ecuador and taken up residence in Quito. Nestled between two ranges of the Andes at nine thousand feet, Quito is South America's second highest capital city. It seemed an appropriate refuge for Julio. The city is shadowed by an awesome twin-cratered volcano, Pichincha. Despite the fact that it straddles the equator and is seething inside with molten lava, Pichincha often is crowned with snow. According to Julio's letter, he was living in a *choza*, a primitive one-room cabin on the slopes of that massive volcano. He begged me to visit him.

Not long afterward, the Ecuadorian government requested a proposal from our company to help organize an industrial park. I volunteered and booked a flight to Quito. I had become disillusioned with my job and decided to take a few days off after the meetings with Ecuadorian officials to spend time with Julio.

I arrived in Quito on a Saturday afternoon, checked into the elegant Hotel Colon, and took a short walk through neighboring El Ejido Park. The air was laden with the scent of eucalyptus. Pichincha loomed above the city. Somewhere on those slopes was Julio's choza. I hoped he had received the letter I had written asking him to join me for Sunday breakfast.

During my Peace Corps days I had spent perhaps a total of two weeks in Quito, spread out over three years. I had always loved this city of beautiful vistas, colonial architecture and glass skyscrapers, wide avenues and crowded Indian markets. I returned from my walk full of happy anticipation. Although the altitude had given me a mild headache, I had the sensation of having come home. I knew that my altitude sickness would be cured by a good night's sleep, and I went to bed early.

I awoke to a clear blue sky. Through the window I could see the snow-capped peak of Pichincha framed between two high-rise office towers. I dressed quickly and hurried to the lobby.

When I stepped off the elevator, there was Julio. The trials of politics and his new life-style had not altered his appearance. Over breakfast, Julio told me he had grown tired of being a lawyer. He was in his mid-fifties now, and wanted time to read and write. His Ecuadorian cousins had arranged a job for him as librarian at Quito's Central University. Money saved from his law practice enabled him to buy the choza on the slopes of the breathtaking volcano.

"Come," he said as we finished our coffee. "You must visit my mountain."

The forests of Pichincha are enchanted. When you leave Quito and travel up the winding mountain trails, you pass from a world of noise into one of silence. In the fragrant eucalyptus groves you hear only birds, small animals, and the occasional Quechua man or woman who greets you in a subdued voice. Whenever you emerge from the shadows you are treated to spectacular views of the city with its red-tiled roofs and cathedral spires, an Incan burial mound rising above the bustling heart of the colonial marketplace, and the gigantic snow-capped volcanoes that guard Quito's perimeter.

Pichincha is but one of the great mountains known in ancient times as "Viracocha's fire-pots." To the Quechua, each is a living presence. Many of Ecuador's volcanoes are active. They are all magnificent. An Indian born in the shadow of any one of the great peaks finds solace in its towering presence. Beginning in early childhood, the mountain becomes as familiar as his mother's face. It is his guardian, a part of his life. He sees it when the sun rises and sets and knows that it watches over him while he sleeps. No matter how far from home his bare feet take him, he can find his way back by looking at the contours of its slopes.

Andean culture abounds with legends about the volcanoes. Cotopaxi takes its name from a youth who saved his tribe from invading armies by transforming himself into a condor and leading his people into the safety of its crater; Cayambi was a giant turtle destroying villages as it clambered out of the Amazon, until Viracocha sent a blizzard to freeze it in its footsteps.

The mountains are a bridge to the eternal. They bring a feeling of inner strength, security, and joy. They are older than time itself. They have always existed and will continue long after the last person has vanished from the face of the earth.

From Pichincha you can see many of the great mountains, and it was to the forests of Pichincha that Julio fled when he was driven from Bolivia. As a boy, he had grown up looking down on La Paz from his home on the slopes of Mount Illimani. For fifteen years he had worked out of an office with a view of the surrounding peaks. It seemed only natural that his second choice for a place to live would be on a mountain overlooking Quito.

The choza was located about a half mile from the end of a dirt road. A bicycle stored in a shed near the road was his transportation to and from his job at the library. After my daily meetings in the city I would take a taxi to the end of the road. That walk to the choza helped me enter Julio's world, a world separated from my own, in both time and distance, by far more than a winding mountain trail up the side of an ancient volcano. My taxi would return at a pre-arranged hour to take me back to the Hotel Colon.

When it became apparent that I would soon complete my series of meetings with Ecuadorian officials and sign a joint venture agreement with a local firm, I mentioned to Julio my intent to vacation in Ecuador.

"Wonderful, John! This choza is tiny. Yes? But we will make room. You must stay with me!"

"But, Julio, this is your private world. My presence would be an intrusion."

"Nonsense! I want to hear more of Indonesia. We must explore psychonavigation together."

The choza was more comfortable than it looked. Julio offered me his cot and slept in a hammock strung across the room. Our water came from a pool in the woods behind us, fed by a crystal spring on the mountain above. Julio had installed a tin chimney over the stone hearth so the air was free of wood smoke. We ate sparingly. He was a superb cook of traditional Ecuadorian soups, made with vegetables, potatoes, avocados, eggs, chicken, rice, and an occasional guinea pig.

We rose early, meditated, and practiced t'ai chi, and ate a light breakfast. Then we wandered along the wooded paths, explored the slopes of Pichincha, or ventured into the city to visit museums. In the evenings we meditated, practiced t'ai chi again, and talked.

Julio had several favorite spots he liked to visit, as he put it, to "gain peace of mind and energize myself." To me it seemed that the mountain was magic. When I was there, I felt relaxed and in harmony with my surroundings. There were two locations I especially liked. The first was nearly an hour's hike from the choza. There, we sat in a clump of trees and looked out on a magnificent view of snow-crowned Cayambi. The other was much nearer. It was a spot on the bank of a brook where wild flowers grew. Julio taught me that places like these could help a person draw in the force of nature during meditation.

"Energy lives also in trees, flowers, and bushes," he said. "Sit near them. Let their aura merge with yours. When you inhale, feel the energy flow in. Do not be afraid to use it. Nature abounds in energy. You cannot deplete it. Only cutting, burning, and bulldozing can do that. Turn trees to paper, asphalt the fields, burn bushes, and you have wasted their energy. But draw that energy into you, make it part of your spirit, and you have added to the greater whole."

One afternoon we arrived at the bank next to the brook I liked so much. In front of us was a bush; scattered throughout its branches were frail yellow flowers. We sat down. "Let's meditate," Julio said.

I had become accustomed to meditating with him and knew his routine. It was similar to what had been taught to me many years earlier by Toyup in Bandung.

I relaxed my body completely, beginning with the toes, and working my way up to my head. Eyes closed, I focused on my breath, feeling it flow throughout me, in and out.

"Now," said Julio quietly, "listen to the brook. Hear it and nothing else."

For many minutes I followed his example. I heard the water rushing over the rocks. The sounds changed constantly, but they were soothing. Despite the changes, there was a reassuring consistency. Occasionally my attention wandered to a bird's call, the breeze in the trees, the sound of a branch falling in the woods, or a dog barking in the distance. Each time, I gently reminded myself to return my attention to the brook. After a while, Julio spoke.

"Now open your eyes and look at the bush in front of you." Slowly,

I did as he instructed. "Pick out a flower." My eyes focused on a tiny yellow blossom close to me. The petals were wilting in the sun and looked fragile. Each had a thin white border framed in yellow. "As you exhale, let out all that is negative. Allow the air to take away any tension. When you breathe in, feel the energy of the flower. It is full of energy. Draw this from it, and let it flow into you. Be aware of the journey this energy takes as it travels through your body. It will reach to every point as it permeates you. Feel it."

I was skeptical, but I tried to do as he instructed. The flower looked so frail. *Try*, I told myself, be positive. Then a strange thing happened.

The flower appeared to change. It opened further, and no longer was wilted. The white border expanded outward, and the yellow grew brighter. As I inhaled, I actually felt its energy flowing into me. I could hardly believe it, and tried to restrain my feelings of joy. Now I could perceive a yellow band—like a halo—beyond the white border, out in the air, in a perfect outline of the flower. I could see the energy! I was very excited, and still it came. There was no question in my mind: I was receiving energy from that flower. After a while, Julio touched my shoulder, and motioned for me to follow him.

The energy stayed with me; it was both physical and mental. As we walked back to the choza, my body felt empowered. The steepest slopes, that before had always left me breathless, required very little effort, and my mind also was affected. Thoughts about the world around me came quickly and with absolute clarity. I mentioned this to Julio.

"Yes," he replied, "you have learned to absorb nature's energy, that is good."

"Julio, I've meditated for years, but I've never experienced anything quite like that!"

"Then be thankful, and don't let go, just keep it up!"

I started to question him further, but he raised a finger to his lips. "Faith, John. Faith and practice!"

One evening Julio and I watched the late afternoon sun paint Cayambi's ice fields golden red. Our side of Pichincha faced east, so we should have been in shadow. Instead, the sun reflecting off Cayambi bathed us in a rosy glow.

Julio stood up and looked toward Cayambi. "Certainly the Egyptians and Persians could have invented mechanical devices to harvest wheat. The Mayas, with their advanced mathematics, must have possessed the ability to build machines to replace many of the jobs assigned to workers. Are we to believe that the warrior nation of the Incas couldn't come up with better weapons than slings, maces, and clubs?"

"What are you suggesting, Julio?"

"They chose not to. You see, all of them had one thing in common. They cherished the earth, worshipped nature. That is where they differed from us. Instead of scheming to subdue the earth, they devoted their energies to living in harmony with her. Theirs was a spiritual orientation. They couldn't conceive of something as destructive as the electric generator or atom bomb."

"You believe that these are collective decisions?"

"Yes. Or, if not collective, at least cultural." He sat down next to me. "One reason I'm so interested in Indonesia is that I see similarities between her people and our own Andean Indians. Despite efforts to persuade the Javanese to mechanize, they prefer to work with their hands. I've read reports, for example, that U.S. and European tractor companies tried to convince Indonesian peasants to replace their water buffaloes with small diesel-powered machines, but the farmers wouldn't do it. Programs in the Andes to persuade the Quechua to form production co-ops and rent machines to carve huge fields out of the mountains have failed time and again. The Quechua prefer to work in family units with their hands. They make small terraces on the slopes, exactly as their ancestors did in Incan times. To the Javanese, the Quechua, and many others—nature is everything. They know what the Egyptians, Greeks, and Persians knew: without earth, water, and air there is nothing. We'd better protect them. Even if a man could survive, his life would be meaningless without them."

"You sound like Don José Quischpe and Buli."

"You see?" He stood and started down the trail. I followed. "Psychonavigators know what they're doing!"

We rounded a corner and came to a spot where the trees opened to a view of three magnificent peaks. One was capped in ice, while the other two were shrouded in clouds. Julio stopped and turned to me. "Look at them, each is separate, until you drop your eyes to the ground beneath; then you know the truth. They are joined by the earth." He spread his arms wide. "All the mountains throughout the world are connected, just as all life is. The lava that erupts from Krakatoa, in Indonesia, shares the fire inside Pichincha. Each is heated by the same source, a vast pool of energy deep inside the earth."

We stood together looking out over the valley at the three volcanoes. The clouds shifted and swirled; as we watched, new clouds materialized behind the third peak. "A storm is brewing," observed Julio. "That summit will be frosted with more snow before morning." He turned to me. "People are like mountains, we are linked to Mother Earth. Although we appear as separate entities, we have much in common. Some call it 'soul,' others 'spirit.' Like the earth's core, we share a source of energy, a vast pool of knowledge. Jung described it as the collective unconscious. Come. I'll show you." Julio started back along the trail to his choza. I glanced at the mountains in the fading light. Dark clouds were creeping down the faces of all three volcanoes. Julio was right about one thing, a fresh blanket of snow would extend far below the normal ice caps by morning.

We reached the choza at sunset. Julio lit two candles and went straight to a leather trunk in the corner. He gently removed an oil lamp, several books, and an Indian tapestry from the top, and set them on a nearby table. Opening the trunk, he quickly found the object of his search.

"A gift," he said, holding out a thick book. "But you must promise not to read it here. You have only two days left in Ecuador. The book is long—wait until you're on the plane. While you are here, concentrate on being here. Promise?"

"Of course." I took the book from him and stepped into the light where I could read the title: Memories, Dreams, Reflections, by C. G. Jung. This famous work was to become a regular companion on my travels and a valuable reference in my inquiries into the nature of human consciousness and the techniques involved in psychonavigating. It would lead me to the Straits of Yucatan where I myself would finally become a psychonavigator.

7

The Straits of Yucatan

What I had thought of as "temporary job burn-out" persisted. In some respects, it seemed more pronounced after my stay with Julio, for now I realized that my consulting work exacted a cost. Although I was traveling a great deal, I was not experiencing the places and people I visited the way I had before. Reading Jung heightened my interest in psychonavigation. This interest was accompanied by diminished enthusiasm for my job. Then, about six months after returning to Boston, I was confronted by a challenge that immersed me in my work.

A fellow manager attempted to increase his territory by reducing mine. He made a bid to absorb my department into his, and we locked horns. At first I fought defensively, seeking only to maintain my turf. When his tactics turned ugly, I took the offensive. I set out to do to him what he was trying to do to me. The battle raged on for nearly a year, engulfing everyone in our two departments and many others who depended on us to assist in their projects. Finally, the president himself intervened. He called us into his office and chewed us out, then ordered us to end the feud and shake hands.

Neither of us won. From a corporate standpoint, everyone lost, because the animosity between the two departments continued. For me, the experience was enlightening; it exposed what I came to view as a serious weakness in the way most corporations function.

The manager who tried to take over my department was the Director of Environmental Planning. I was Director of Economic Planning and Management Consulting. On many projects, his department and mine were supposed to work closely together to assure that economic benefits could be realized without disrupting the environment, or with as little disruption as possible. As we became locked in a power struggle, this goal became secondary to the selfish aims of two corporate warriors motivated solely by ego. Ours was a struggle having nothing whatsoever to do with serving the interests of our clients, the environment, the corporation, or society as a whole. Unfortunately, it is not atypical.

After it was over, I became deeply concerned by the implications of this incident; at times I was very depressed. Influenced by Jung's book, I sought the help of a psychologist named Bernie.

"Listen to your heart," Bernie said. "Open up to your emotions. Let your inner self speak to you." How like Don José and Toyup he sounded!

One day Bernie helped me recall a painful event from my early childhood. I actually relived it as though there were two of me: the man sitting next to Bernie, and the child. Eventually, Bernie brought the child into the present. Before the session ended, he asked if I had been aware of a stutter when I spoke. I had not been. Then something I had completely forgotten about dawned on me; for a brief period during my childhood, I had stuttered.

"You forgot, but the subconscious remembers," said Bernie.

As I walked down the street to catch the train back to my office, I wondered if my experience had been a kind of psychonavigation. I had never attempted to do that which I had spent so much time studying; now I began to consider it as a distinct possibility. I also fully understood that my job had become a very heavy burden. "Soft profitables" were in demand. My department sent people all over the world, and I was getting rich. By all objective standards I should have been happy; I was not.

While shaving one morning, I glimpsed an image from my past looking out at me; my 1968 business school professor. "Take nature into account as you scale the ladders of corporate America," he seemed to say. My sessions with Bernie helped me place such experiences in perspective. Much of the work I was doing was contrary to my deepest beliefs. My company was engineering hydroelectric dams in virgin forests, building roads into the Amazon, and industrial parks in the high Andes. What were we doing to people like the Shuara and Quechua? One of our clients was constructing a concrete manufacturing plant outside Quito. How many brickmakers would starve as a result?

On my next visit with Bernie, I tried to convince us both that I should stay with my job and attempt to make changes from within the system. He encouraged me to talk it out, then asked the critical question. "Was that the voice of your heart, John, or was it your head trying to manipulate your heart?"

I strolled into my boss's office the following day and told him I needed a month off. I would spend it in Mexico's Yucatan, visiting Mayan friends.

To my surprise, he acquiesced. "We all get burned out every now and then," he said. "Just agree to two things: make sure all your bases are covered while you're away; and promise me you'll return refreshed, rejuvenated, and ready to make money."

I felt relieved at avoiding a confrontation. I could go to Mexico and still keep my job. My stock would continue earning dividends. It was almost too good to be true! I agreed to his two conditions, and headed off to Mexico a week later. I would have a whole month free from the demands of my job to reorder my priorities, and I would be in the Yucatan. I never guessed that before returning to Boston I would take several extraordinary psychonavigational journeys.

The Mayan fishermen who met for a beer in the late afternoon at Cantina El Rincon on Isla Mujeres, off the coast of Mexico's Yucatan Peninsula, tried to persuade me not to sail to Key West aboard a thirty-three-foot wooden sloop named *Kaos*. But my leave of absence was nearly over, and I was not yet ready to return to my job in Boston. One more adventure was just what I needed!

"You'll be blown out of the water by Cuban gunboats!"

"If you don't die of seasickness first. The Straits are no place for a landlubber!"

"How do you know these 'pirates' aren't smuggling drugs?"

"You'll end up in a Florida jail!"

I left Cantina El Rincon and strolled down to the beach. The half moon cast a silver trail across the Caribbean. *Kaos* was riding at anchor; orange light shone through her portholes. Seeing her there in the moonlight gave me a warm feeling. A voice inside told me to do it. Despite the logic of the fishermen, I knew my decision was right.

My month in the Yucatan had been much like that. I had acted on impulse. Although my intention had been to visit Viejo Itza* and other

_____

* See my first book, *The Stress Free Habit* (Rochester, Vermont: Healing Arts Press, 1989).

Mayan friends, I had never even made it to one of the many archaeological sites I loved. I stayed a week in Merida, lounging by a hotel pool, reading, writing in my journal, and treating myself to wonderful food and lots of beer. It had felt like the right thing to do. After a week I went directly to Isla Mujeres. Three weeks of snorkeling, night life, reading, writing, eating, and drinking, passed too quickly. Every now and then I had a twinge of guilt. I tried to convince myself that I should take the ferry back to the mainland and find my way out to Viejo Itza's village. "Stop being so damned indolent," I lectured myself. "It's time to get moving and be productive!" But another voice persuaded me to do just what I was doing. "Listen to your heart," Bernie had said. I followed his advice. This was a new experience for me and it felt wonderful.

The next morning I was on the beach again. I met *Kaos'* dinghy and helped Rob, the boat's owner, and his friend Steve pull *Little Kaos* up on the beach.

"Well, are you with us?" Rob asked. They had sailed in from Panama two days earlier. Exhausted by a violent storm, they were looking for people to stand watch during a five day sail to Florida. Judy and Barbara, two University of Chicago students trying to save airfare, had already agreed. Neither they nor I had ever spent a night at sea, but it didn't seem to matter to Rob and Steve.

"I'm with you," I replied. I felt wildly elated.

"Did you see that wave?" Judy's eyes were wide as she turned to me. I wondered if my terror showed as much as hers.

"Yeah. But it didn't feel nearly as bad as it looked." I wanted desperately to sound brave. Perhaps, I could even fool myself!

"We're on a sleigh ride through an ocean gorge," Steve explained from his perch behind the wheel. The seas had grown progressively worse during the three hours since our departure from Isla Mujeres. Dark clouds threatened to open up at any moment. "This is a branch of the Gulf Stream that gets squeezed between Mexico, Cuba, and the States. Sure, the waves are big, but it's more than their size; it's the way they hit from every angle. Just when you think you know what's coming—wham—one broadsides your ass from out of nowhere."

Judy rolled her eyes. Barbara, stretched straight out on top of the cabin, groaned.

"If you feel queasy," Steve spoke to no one in particular, "don't go below. The world is topsy-turvy down in that cabin. Stay here. Air's good!"

"How come you and Rob spend so much time down there?"

"Oh, that's different. We're used to it. Ocean's in our blood now. When John had the wheel, I was below feasting on pickled herring and peanut butter."

"Shut up, Steve! For God's sake." Judy pulled her knees up to her chin and hugged them. "Don't even mention food!" Her eyes were glassy, her face white as the sails. Suddenly she glanced at me with a panicky expression as though she suddenly remembered something she had left behind on Isla Mujeres. Then in one wrenching move-ment, she turned away from the cockpit and leaned over the side of the boat.

"Oh, oh," said Steve. "One down." He leaned towards her, keeping one hand on the wheel; with the other he gently patted her shoulder. "Just let it come. Get it all out of your system. Don't forget to hold onto the railing, though. Very important, mate. Don't want anyone overboard."

Barbara sat up and peered at Judy. Slowly and with cautious deliberation, she crawled off the cabin like a crab onto the deck near her friend. Then, she too, leaned her head over the side.

"When it rains, it pours." Steve shook his head. He turned to me. "You okay?"

"Sure." But as soon as I said it, I knew it was not true. An acrid, nauseating taste filled my mouth. My stomach clawed at my throat.

"Don't fight it."

Could this be happening on my last great adventure before returning to the workaday world? I mustered all my dignity, as I tried to step across the cockpit. The wind was blowing from my side of the boat (I took comfort in the knowledge that I was still able to notice this). "Never spit into the wind," somebody in a novel had said that. Then I lost my balance and lurched forward, and landed in a sprawl next to Barbara. I glanced up at Steve. To my relief, he was looking up, and forward. Perhaps he was studying the set of the sail. Or maybe he was just being considerate. Soon I was too ill to care. I too leaned over the side. Never before in my life had I been so violently sick.

After some time, I felt a hand on my shoulder. "Try to sit up. That's my advice."

I had heard that seasickness makes people wish they were dead. Now I knew it was only a slight exaggeration. My head throbbed. My stomach felt like a snake pit, and everything ached. My eyes refused to focus.

With a painful effort, I managed to pull myself into a half-sitting position. The mast reeled as if it would topple into the hissing waves. Rob's face spun around in dizzying circles. Everything was distorted as though a thick haze had invaded the cockpit. I told myself that my mind was playing tricks. I concentrated until my eyes began to focus. Rob's face stabilized. He was leaning over me, smiling. Steve was still perched behind the wheel. How long had I been like this? Between the clouds the sky was now rosy; it was already sunset. Barbara and Judy were still leaning over the side next to me. One of them moaned.

"Your watch is at two in the morning," Rob said into my ear. "We need you to take the helm. Try to get some sleep. But I wouldn't go below if I were you." He handed me a blanket.

There was a quick rush of bile to my throat. I turned and threw up over the side. Rob's voice sounded faint. "Perhaps you won't make your watch after all. Well, Steve, this is one hell of a crew we found ourselves!"

I heard Steve laugh, and felt ashamed, then angry. I tried to concentrate on the waves slamming against the side of the boat. I did not want to be sick any longer. I stared into the boiling ocean, afraid that my anger would find expression through my stomach. My ears rang with Rob's words, and Steve's laughter.

Looking into the waves, I thought of Captain Joshua Slocum, the first person to circumnavigate the globe by himself. In his book, *Sailing Alone Around the World*, he had described the type of psychonavigation experience I needed right now. While in a sick delirium, he was visited by what I have come to call an Inner Pilot. While Slocum remained in his cabin, too ill to tend to the boat, his Pilot stood at the wheel, singing sea chanties and guiding the sloop through a gale.

Despite my numerous encounters with people who practiced psychonavigation, I had never attempted it myself. Perhaps it was embarrassment that had kept me from participating. Perhaps it was my staunch New England background, or fear of failure. Seeing the waves swirling below me, I decided that the time had come.

My research had confirmed that what was practiced by the Shuara, Birdmen, and Bugis was real. They had learned to accomplish something vital, powerful, and wonderful. They were human beings who had fully integrated their minds and bodies in a way that is harmonious with the natural environment. I knew that all of us, if we go back far enough, have roots in cultures where psychonavigation once played an important role. It is part of our heritage and one of our birthrights as human beings.

Slowly I sat up. My thoughts returned to Captain Slocum. Like the Shuara, Quechua, and Bugis he had called upon a guide for assistance, an Inner Pilot. Instead of a jaguar or bird, his had been a man, which is often the case in cultures where deities are perceived in human form.

For what seemed like hours, I sat quietly in the cockpit. Sometimes I felt Steve's eyes studying me curiously. The sound of his mocking laughter still rang in my ears. Inner pilots plot courses for psychonavigation. I stood up, clutched the handrail on the outside of the companionway, and started down into the cabin.

"Don't go below, unless you want to die, mate." Steve laughed once again.

I placed my right foot on the top stair and peered into the darkness. Beside a tiny light near the chart table, Rob's face turned towards me.

"What the hell are you doing?"

When I arrived at the bottom, I headed forward. In the bow was a V-berth. It is, sailors will tell you, the roughest spot on a boat. Those prone to seasickness should avoid it. Clutching the railings along each side of the cabin for balance, I moved directly to the V-berth. I reached it, kicked off my tennis shoes, and lay down.

The sound of the heavy seas pounding into the boat was deafening. Every fiber of the small vessel seemed to groan from the effort of staying afloat. When a wave struck, the bow shuddered as if it had been rammed by a bulldozer. Water dripped from somewhere above my head.

"Hey," Rob shouted into my ear. "If you insist on being crazy, keep this near." He handed me the open end of a plastic garbage bag.

I nodded, and tried to smile at him. He staggered away, and I repeated over and over the words: Inner Pilots. I thought about psychonavigation. Unlike Captain Slocum, I did not need to find my way in a physical sense. My need was an internal one, to explore the inner recesses of my being and find the place where mind, body, and spirit come together. If I could do that, I could find a state of equilibrium where the seasickness would go away. "Ocean's in our blood now," Steve had said. Well, I figured, it could get into mine too.

I could feel the full impact of *Kaos's* movements. The little boat pitched up and forward, then lurched violently to the side. I needed my Inner Pilot. I had studied psychonavigation long enough. When would I encounter a better laboratory for testing my theories? Lying there, as far forward in the boat as I could get, I finally let myself go. I didn't care what would happen next. I dropped the plastic bag. So what if I vomited! But I knew I would not. I knew, as surely as the sound of the sea outside, that an Inner Pilot would come to me. I relaxed totally, and absolutely let myself go. I closed my eyes and released everything from my mind. The sounds around me flooded in and washed back out. I focussed on the air passing into my lungs. Then I listened to the ocean pounding against the hull. Suddenly, the sea was all around me. "Please come," I said. "I need your help. Please."

Then she appeared; everything stopped. Before me stood a beautiful woman with long blond hair, dressed like she had just arrived from ancient Greece. She held out her hand and I took it. What I felt was pure energy—not like the touch of a human hand, but nonetheless very real. She pulled me forward and the boat seemed to grow around us. She then led me on a tour of *Kaos*, traveling down into the keel, up the mast, and along the high rigging. The sounds of the wood, wind, and waves were loud and distinct. I could feel the texture of the wood and the steel fittings as we glided past them. It was an incredible journey, oddly familiar, completely natural, as though I had done this many times before. My Inner Pilot never spoke. She simply led the way and pointed at the turnbuckles in the stays, the gooseneck where mast and boom were joined, and the heavy plates anchoring the mast to the keel. I had never studied these things before, but their purpose was now perfectly clear to the last detail. Later when I examined them closely, I found them to be exactly as I had seen them during our voyage.

When we returned, I felt peaceful and at one with the boat. The plunging and pitching, banging and creaking made sense to me for the first time. What had terrified me before was now comforting, for I understood the way *Kaos* utilized the elements to her advantage instead of being torn apart by them. The boat was like a living being. It constantly adapted to these outside forces, expanding and contracting, yawing and rolling in order to compensate for the pressures of wind and water. When my guide left, she simply waved good-bye. I thanked her, and moved to the edge of the berth.

Rob came below at 2 A.M. I was sitting there on the edge of the V-berth tying my shoelaces. The little light above my head illumined his face. He looked like a man watching a corpse rise up from the grave.

"Unbelievable," was all he said, then he turned back toward the companionway and motioned for me to come along.

As I followed Rob up the companionway into the cockpit, I was euphoric. The night was dark and windy. I might have felt threatened by the sound of the waves hissing and snarling along the hull and the wind howling in the spars, but instead I experienced a sense of blissful happiness. I knew that *Kaos* would make it, and so would I. The seasickness was over, and deep down inside, I understood that something very special had happened.

During the next four hours I was alone on deck. The two girls were in berths in the aft cabin, and each had a plastic, seasickness bag. Rob and Steve had to share the V-berth in the bow. When my eyes became accustomed to the darkness, I could see the stars as they appeared briefly between the swirling clouds. Once, I caught a glimpse of the moon. Rob had trimmed *Kaos's* sails and they required no changes during my watch. But the wheel had a lot of play, and I had to stay on my toes to keep her sailing along the desired compass course.

The early morning light revealed seas as violent as they had been the previous afternoon, but my body's reaction to them was entirely different. Apart from being tired, I felt fine.

Steve stuck his head through the companionway. "How you feeling?"

"Wonderful."

He studied me carefully, and muttered something inaudible. Then hoisted himself into the cockpit. He peered into the east where the burnished glow in the clouds along the horizon indicated sunrise.

"She'll burn off today for sure. We'll get sun all right. Good day for tanning."

"I hope you're right."

He stepped behind the wheel. "My turn now," he said taking it from me. "Hope the girls have as good a recovery as you, mate. Miraculous, I'd say. Why don't you go below and get some sleep?"

"I'm starved. Can I fix you breakfast?"

"Better watch yourself. Don't go testing your luck. Get cocky and you'll find yourself sick again."

"All the same, I'm going to cook up some beans and rice. Want any?"

"If you insist, mate. Never refused beans and rice before. Why start now? And how 'bout brewing some fresh coffee while you're at it? That stuff Ron filled the thermos with is strong enough to kill a horse."

"Sure." I started down the companionway, then stopped and turned to look at him. He was unshaven, his hair was dishevelled, and his lean body was bronzed by the sun. He looked like the saltiest of sailors. "Ever read Joshua Slocum?"

"Who?"

"Slocum. Wrote a book called *Sailing Alone Around the World.*"

"Oh, that one. Nope, can't say as I have. Seen it though, lying around. I think Rob's got a copy. Any good?"

"Great. Read it next time you come across it, at least the part about Slocum's sickness."

"That'd interest you more than me." His laugh was friendly this time. I went below to cook up rice and beans and brew a fresh pot of coffee.

Later that morning the sun broke through. Except for an occasional shower or line squall, the next three days were clear. The seas, however, continued to be rough and unpredictable. As a consequence, Barbara and Judy never fully recovered until we reached Key West. They were mystified by my transformation, and, I suspect, rather envious. At one point I tried to explain about Inner Pilots and how to become one with the boat, but I was a lousy teacher. Under the circumstances, they were not exactly receptive students, so I dropped the subject. It was enough to know that it had worked for me. Watching them, I knew that without psychonavigation, I too would be listless on the deck, always at the edge of violent seasickness. Instead, I had a wonderful three days and an experience that would change my life forever.

I disembarked from *Kaos* and stayed in Key West for another three days. I was too elated to return to my job in Boston right away. How could I concentrate at a desk? I had at last psychonavigated. Something gnawed at me inside. I sensed there was more to come and knew there were unanswered questions I needed to address.

Finally, on the third day, I made reservations for the next morning. I would take a bus to Miami, and fly to Boston. That last afternoon I walked down to the beach and stood at the edge of the water watching the sun slide into a silvery sea. I knew something was about to happen. Then I felt her presence; the sensation was unmistakable.

I lay down on the sand, closed my eyes, and relaxed deeply. I repeated the steps I had taken in *Kaos's* V-berth. For a very long time, nothing happened. Then I saw dim lights that evolved into stars. I felt myself lift up and head into them. It was then that my Inner Pilot appeared, the same beautiful lady who had come to me aboard *Kaos*. She led me out over the Caribbean on a voyage that was enjoyable and instructive. This time she talked to me. I found I could ask questions about my life and she would reply. Her answers were well thought out and direct. By the time I returned, I knew exactly what steps I should take to realize a lifelong dream.

When I returned to Boston in late February, the annual New England Boat Show was in full swing. I was only mildly surprised for I was learning that once an Inner Pilot helps set a course, things tend to fall into place. I spent most of that weekend examining a seemingly endless array of sailing vessels. I questioned dozens of manufacturers' representatives, and talked with many brokers.

During the following week, I left the office in the evenings and visited the docks along Lewis Wharf and Constitution Marina. I spoke with the handful of intrepid sailors who lived aboard their sailboats through the long, cold New England winter. I carried a six-pack of beer and cheerfully accepted invitations into their cabins, and examined every conceivable sort of rig for protecting cockpits and hulls against the snow and ice. I took notes and asked questions.

What type of heater did they recommend? How did they guard against fire? What about insurance?

I was living at the time in a beautiful Boston apartment. Spacious and light, twenty-six floors above Tremont Street, it had two bedrooms and a living room with picture windows that looked out over The Boston Common. I could see Beacon Hill, the gold-domed State House, the Charles River, and Cambridge in the distance. It was the embodiment of a New Hampshire milltown boy's fantasy: elegant, luxurious, and glamorous.

In the early morning, I would rise and stretch, and then lie down on a carpet I had purchased in Iran, and call to my Inner Pilot. Sometimes we simply talked. In the process, I found answers to the questions I had asked myself. Often my guide led me on journeys that enlightened me in ways words could not.

It was during this period that I began framing my own approach to psychonavigation—one I have used ever since. The keys, I discovered, are faith that the process will work and an ability to relax the mind and body totally. I have also found it important to ask my Inner Pilot to join me and to thank him or her when the session is over. Whenever doubts or inhibitions intrude, the necessary "state" is broken and the process is interrupted. In the beginning of my practice, this happened frequently because I was self-conscious and somewhat worried about what I was doing; at the time, I knew no one else in the United States who psychonavigated. I sometimes wondered whether I was going off the deep end, but in my heart I knew I was not. Thinking of the Shuara, the Bugis, the Quechua, Don José, and Julio Sinchi reassured me.

During the two months following the end of the boat show, I devoted every free minute to my search for a boat. I traveled the New England coast, from Maine to Rhode Island. Few sailboats between twenty-eight and thirty-five feet in length escaped my scrutiny. Finally, in May 1979, I bought one: a thirty-foot sloop made in Bristol, Rhode Island. She had a white hull, and green decks. I named her *Tamara*, after a character in a novel I had begun. Within six months of returning from the Yucatan, I had moved out of my elegant two bedroom apartment onto a tiny sailboat docked in Boston Harbor!

Less than ten months after *Kaos's* landfall in Key West, I assembled my own crew of three and headed *Tamara* out into the Atlantic. We sailed from Boston to Charleston, South Carolina. The voyage lasted sixteen days. We hit weather so rough it made the Yucatan Straits seem tame when we sailed into a tornado off the coast of Delaware, and were engulfed in winds clocked by the Coast Guard at over 100 miles per hour. But we all made it, and eventually sailed back to Boston.

I was thirty-four years old. My lifestyle was the envy of other bachelors. I had traveled all over the world and dated many women.

On Fourth of July weekend I sat on *Tamara's* deck and looked across Boston Harbor from my berth in Constitution Marina at the steeple of the old North Church where Paul Revere's lantern had warned of a British march. Despite my wonderful boat and what objectively appeared to be a fantastic life, I felt terribly alone and sad. For the first time I knew that I did not want to be a permanent bachelor. I wanted to love someone and be loved. I desired a commitment. I wanted a soulmate and a child—at least one. The sad thing was that, as I thought about all the women I knew and had known for most of my life, I also realized that none of them—not a single one—was a person with whom I wanted to spend my life. There had been good friendships and exceptional love affairs, but never anyone vaguely resembling a soulmate. Then I recalled another Fourth of July—the one I'd spent in Sulawesi. Thoughts of Buli and the Bugi shipbuilders filled my mind. I felt much better and knew that it was time to take control.

I went below. I crawled into the forward V-berth and lay there, feeling *Tamara* rise and fall with the waves. Then I called on my Inner Pilot. Quickly she came. She was radiant. She gently touched my arm. Then she beckoned for me to follow her up through the deck and over the top of my boat's mast. We hovered there, suspended above the harbor. The lights of Boston twinkled around us.

"Now," she said, "John, you are feeling very sleepy. Don't resist. Fall asleep." Immediately I did so.

I saw a young lady whom I recognized as an engineer. Her name was Winifred and she had recently come to work in another department at my company. I had been introduced to her, and chatted politely with her. Now, in my dream, I approached her. "The best ice cream in Boston," I said to her, "is at a little shop up on Beacon Hill near the State House." She reached out and took my hand. "Let's go," she said.

"Follow your dream," my Inner Pilot whispered. Suddenly I felt myself falling. I sat up with a start and hit my head on the bottom of the foredeck which was the V-berth ceiling.

The next morning, rather sheepishly, I approached Winifred's desk. I recognized the suit as the one she had worn in my dream, and it gave me courage. She looked up and smiled in a kind, friendly way.

"Excuse me for interrupting," I said, trying to appear as confident as a department manager should. "I hope you won't think me forward, but I have something rather funny to tell you."

She asked me to sit down and I told her about my dream, leaving out the part about my Inner Pilot. I finished by saying, "and I don't even know if you like ice cream."

"I love ice cream," she laughed. Then she had to take a phone call.

Later that afternoon, she dropped by my office. "Where did you say you keep your boat?"

"Constitution Marina."

"Isn't that in Charlestown?"

"Yes."

"After work I have appointments to look at several apartments in Charlestown. Perhaps you can tell me about the area. . . ."

My days as a bachelor were numbered. Within two years after my first personal experience with psychonavigation, Winifred and I had married; I had also quit my job, and we had sailed *Tamara* from Boston to Florida. We decided to move to Palm Beach and start a family, and our daughter Jessica was born on May 17, 1982.

8

Roof of the World

"You are going to hear a lot about psychonavigation in the future. If you should have the misfortune of contracting a serious disease or developing an addiction, you will probably be asked to include psychonavigation as part of the cure."

I looked up from the draft of the speech I would give when I returned to the United States in a week. Through the windows of the hotel bar, "Roof of the World," the lights of Quito twinkled in the Andean night. Winifred was two floors below tucking six-year-old Jessica into bed. She would rejoin me any minute now. I hurried on with my review.

"You have heard two remarkable stories tonight. In one, the Birdmen of the Andes traveled beyond time to communicate with their ancestors. In the other, an Inner Pilot helped me understand what was going on in the structure of a small sailboat and, by dispelling my fear, conquer my seasickness. These stories are remarkable only because we in the West are not accustomed to hearing them. Fortunately this is changing.

"Modern medicine has begun to understand the benefits of psychonavigation. Techniques stemming from this ancient practice are today being used in hospitals throughout the world to fight drug abuse, cancer, hemophilia, heart disease, and even to mend broken bones. Relaxation and meditation are often combined with visual-ization techniques to help the patient travel deep inside his or her body and psyche. Two branches of medical science, *cyberbiology* and *cyberphysiology*, have been particularly successful at helping people use such methods to discover the causes of their ailments and to initiate cures. It is interesting to note that the root of the names of these two sciences, *cyber*, is taken from the Greek *kybernam*, meaning 'to navigate.'"

I glanced out the window once again, thinking about the similarities between people who are taught by U.S. doctors to visualize friendly forces attacking their illnesses* and the Shuara who attune with their jaguar-god. Here I was, back in Ecuador, more than twenty years after Tanya and Bomi first predicted the destruction of the jungle. Quito was the city where I spent those precious days with Julio. It had expanded and modernized, but it was still a place of contrasts—where sixteenth century Spanish cathedrals, glass skyscrapers, and open air markets were all juxtaposed—a place I loved.

Psychonavigation had become an important part of my life. It had been a major factor in so many decisions. During the past six years it had helped me understand the environmental problems threatening our planet and our existence as a species. A first step had been the Pennsylvania culm-burning project. On impulse I flipped ahead in the speech and read:

"The Pennsylvania project was truly a pioneering effort. Nothing of its type had been built before. The technology was unproven. No facility like it had ever been financed. During the three years it took to get the financing needed for construction, I encountered every conceivable obstacle including an unexpected and potentially devastating change in the tax laws. Time and again I turned to psychonavigation for solutions. It was my source of energy and inner strength. It enabled me to take advantage of resources deep within my own subconscious.

"I was following in the footsteps of notables from many fields. The list of psychonavigators includes some very famous people: scientists such as Einstein, Burbank, Marconi, and Edison; musicians including Bach, Beethoven, Schumann, and Mozart; writers such as Keats, Shelly, and Joyce; even political leaders such as Roosevelt, Gandhi, and Kennedy. There are fascinating stories about Winston Churchill's reliance on his Inner Pilots to guide his activities. One is a well-documented account of an episode in London during 1941 when an Inner Pilot directed him away from a spot where a German bomb exploded seconds later."

My immediate concern now was the global destruction threatening

---

* See for example "Cyberphysiology in Children." *Advances: Journal of the Institute for the Advancement of Health,* Vol. 5, Number 4.

the magical combination of air, water, and earth capable of sustaining life as we know it. Unlike the literal bombs of terrorism and nuclear warfare, this was something pervasive, and far more frightening.

I reached for my beer, wondering what had detained Winifred. Probably she and Jessica were lying on a bed below peering out the window, infatuated by a scene reminiscent of fairy tales. I looked out on a panorama that included the entire valley. At night, the bright stars seemed mirrored in the street lights below. Only the massive hump of Pichincha itself was shrouded in darkness.

I had enjoyed this view many times, as a Peace Corps Volunteer, tourist, management consultant, and advisor to the World Bank. Most of my work had been devoted to helping the country improve its economy or set up management structures to facilitate development, but now my role was different.

I was 44 years old and a father. I had recently held a number of important talks with myself, concluding that much of my life had been rather selfish. I had made a good living, traveled, and learned a lot. However, I had often ignored voices deep within that questioned the true benefits of building another industrial park or oil-fired generating plant. I hated to admit it, but I had taken the easy way out, assuming that others were to blame for the world's ills.

"*They* study these things," I had told myself and anyone else who would listen. "*They* have compared the benefits of $500 million invested in a power plant with the same amount devoted to agriculture. *They* know. I am here to see to it that the management systems are in place to support *their* investment."

It was always they. It was up to them to protect the environment, watch out for the poor, and defend Indian cultures. I had entered the Peace Corps, John Kennedy's brainchild, and later worked for Robert McNamara (Secretary of Defense under Kennedy and, later, President of the World Bank). I had advised Heads of State. Famous politicians and corporate executives had paid handsomely for my counsel; I believed in these people and their successors. I had assumed they were making the right decisions.

Recently, I had seen the folly in this. My conversations with myself had begun to sound different. "Could it be that they make mistakes like you? Or even that *you* are *they*?" I had come to understand that someone looking at me might view me as one of *them*. I was successful, I had been around, and had advised some very important people. In fact, I had played a key role in many of *their* decisions.

I began a series of dialogues with my Inner Pilots. I learned much about my own feelings toward others, my relationships to *them*, and how I might be viewed vis-à-vis my role as one of them.

In some respects these government, political, business, and social leaders had come a long way since I first visited Ecuador in 1968. Poised to enter the last decade of the twentieth century, they were bombarded by stories of the destruction of the Amazon. Tanya's terrible vision had come true not only in the region around El Milagro, but also in Brazil, Peru, the Philippines, and many other countries. Pictures of a devastated earth had been flashed across TV screens around the world. Deforestation and slash-and-burn agriculture posed a widespread threat because of their contribution to the Greenhouse Effect. Wall Street lawyers, Senate candidates, utility executives, and Midwestern bankers had joined with Amazonian Indians to express their concern.

From another viewpoint, no progress whatsoever had been made. In fact, development had succeeded only in causing further damage to our planet. World population had skyrocketed from one billion in 1800 to two billion in 1930. It had doubled again by 1975, and was continuing to double every forty years. Per capita consumption had increased at exponential rates, and we were poisoning the rivers, air, and land. We were wantonly depleting our natural resources, and irreparably polluting the biosphere.

I could pick up any magazine or newspaper on any given day in 1989, and see that *they* were doing a lousy job. It also was apparent that if something were not done quickly, six-year-old Jessica would face an increasingly ugly world. The question of whether or not I was one of them had become academic; I could not ignore the simple fact that I damn well had better try to do something. The longer I thought about it, the more I understood the truth of it. Compared to a commitment to do all I could to protect Mother Earth, all the other things I might be able to offer Jessica were trivial. What good are swimming lessons if the oceans are contaminated?

9

Alpha

Our planet is threatened not by external forces, but by us. Humanity's current path is one that leads to environmental disaster. Despite our attempts to use science to convince ourselves otherwise, we know this is true. The evidence is everywhere. All our senses tell us so, and we can feel it in our hearts.

Our decision-making process may utilize objective information and scientific analysis. Yet, ultimately, all choices are made by people who draw on inner resources. Even the most "objective" scientist must rely on intuitive judgments to help in the selection of data and the formulation of hypotheses. There is within each of us a vast pool of knowledge. Jung called it the "collective unconscious." We often employ it when we make decisions. We describe a person particularly skilled at this with words like: "insightful," "wise," "brilliant," and "enlightened."

Psychonavigation provides a tool for accessing this universal knowledge. Jung himself psychonavigated frequently. He explained the phenomenon as an inner journey into the realm of the collective unconscious. By entering this realm he was able to draw on the awesome body of information that is equally available to people living in the heart of jungles, on the slopes of the Himalayas, in African deserts, and in modern cities.

Human history is a collage of our decisions. The choices we have made during the past two centuries have created a serious threat to our planet; it is time for us to choose anew. Psychonavigation can enable us to better understand our current position. By letting us reach down into this well of knowledge, it can show us how to make decisions that will allow us to chart another course. We know we have a problem. We can find solutions. It is important to understand the techniques that are available to help us in our task. The techniques have been proven time and time again. They were used by our ancestors. They ignited the brilliance of people like Edison, Marconi, Einstein, Gandhi, and Churchill. They are used today by medical doctors, scientists, artists, business leaders, and people from many other walks of life.

Several theories have been advanced to explain psychonavigation, including ones involving genetics and morphogenetic fields.* Whether we favor these or Jung's theory of the collective unconscious is not really important. What matters is that it works as a tool to help us get in touch with an essential part of ourselves, a place where our physical, mental, and spiritual energies can be focused to help us be more creative, healthier, and at peace with ourselves. It is safe, enjoyable, and relatively easy to learn.

I have found only one ingredient essential for psychonavigation. Shamans deep in the Amazon, Bugis designing ships in Sulawesi, Birdmen flying off to visit their ancestors in the high Andes, and Fortune 500 executives taking the inner journey to increased pro-ductivity—all share this trait: In order to psychonavigate, you must have a positive attitude. It is the sole prerequisite, and a principle whose importance has been recognized throughout the ages.

The next step is to learn a fundamental technique for psycho-navigation. The objective is to attain the alpha state, a scientifically measurable condition during which the frequency of brain waves is reduced.

Children tend to spend significantly more time operating in the alpha state than adults do. Many researchers believe this is why childhood is often called the "formative period." Alpha is a mind state that is open and receptive to new information. Our learning and creative faculties are at their peak. We are awake and alert, yet our brain wave activity has slowed to a level that allows us to tune in to our subconscious and unconscious mind. Although the alpha state can be produced during physical activity—the Birdman ceremony for example—most people find that relaxation techniques are the best practice for entering alpha.

The following pages outline a method to help you voluntarily trigger the alpha state. If you have already learned progressive relaxation or

* See for example Rupert Sheldrake, *A New Science of Life: the Hypothesis of Formative Causation* (Jeremy P. Tarcher, Inc., Los Angeles, 1987).

some other meditative technique, the steps outlined below will be easy to follow. If not, you may have to practice them, but the results will be well worth the effort. Not only will they help you enter a state from which you may contact your own Inner Pilots, but they will also help you become relaxed very quickly whenever you need to.

These steps are fun and extremely beneficial. You will discover that regular use of these techniques can help lower your rate of breathing, metabolism, pulse, and blood pressure. All of these occurrences are scientifically measurable. They help promote physical as well as emotional health. You will soon find that you have entered a state from which you can begin to psychonavigate.

If you suffer from any physical or psychological condition, these techniques may also hold real therapeutic potential; however, they should be followed only with the approval of a physician.

Here then are the steps in the basic approach:

1. *Find a quiet and peaceful place.* It is a matter of personal preference whether you chose a dark corner, a window with a view, or somewhere in between. Ideally, the environment should calm you. It should be free from distractions (conversations, telephones, barking dogs, playing children) as much as possible.

2. *Sit in a comfortable position.* Sit in a favorite chair with your feet flat on the floor, or sit cross-legged on the floor. You do not have to learn any special techniques; just make sure you are comfortable. I do not recommend lying down since the temptation of drowsiness is too great. I prefer sitting cross-legged on the floor with my back against a wall, couch, or bed.

3. *Relax.* Just let your body go. Be aware of your muscles, and consciously feel the tension flow out of them. This should not be a demanding effort; let it be natural and pleasant. At this point don't concentrate on relaxing specific parts of the body; rather, simply "let your body go." Release the tension. Make sure that your spine is in correct alignment so that respiratory and digestive functions are not impeded. In other words, while your muscles should relax, your skeleton should not slouch. Close your eyes and keep them closed.

4. *Take a deep breath.* Breathe in through your nose, gently hold the air in your lungs for several seconds, then exhale slowly through

your mouth. Feel good about yourself. Let positive feelings flow throughout your body. Repeat the deep breathing. Feel the strength of a positive attitude as the air enters your nose, flows downward to your chest, passes from the lungs into the bloodstream, and permeates every cell of your body. Allow the exhaled air to be a carrier of all your misgivings. Positive energy and belief—in yourself, your religion, an idea, or a goal—enters with each inhalation; and doubts are cleansed with each exhalation. In and out. Repeat this breathing cycle several times. You may experience a sensation of being rejuvenated, but do not deliberately try to attain this sensation, and do not be disturbed if it does not happen. Just concentrate on your breathing and breathe in the flow of positive energy.

5. *Relax completely.* Let your body relax as you did in step 3, but this time concentrate on specific parts of the body. Feel each part, and consciously relax it. It may help to tense a muscle first, then relax it. I start with my toes, wiggle them, and then let them go until they are completely relaxed. Then I do the same for the rest of my feet. Relax your ankles, calves, and so on, all the way up to your shoulders and down each arm to your fingers, tensing first and then relaxing. Then relax your back, your neck, the parts of your face: mouth, cheeks, eyes, ears, forehead. Finally, relax the top and the back of your head.

Let your mind totally relax; think about nothing. If you find this difficult, concentrate on a single word such as your name, or "peace," "love," "God," or simply "one." When your mind wanders, gently remind it not to. Don't be tough on yourself. Other thoughts will intrude. Simply return to no thoughts or to concentration on your word.

This step takes practice. If you have not done it before, you may discover that it requires more time than you expected. Be patient. With a little practice, it will come easily and quickly. In a short time, it will be almost instantaneous.

You should now be in the alpha state and ready to enter the realm of psychonavigation.

6. *Feel your inner self beginning to move.* There are numerous options here. You may enjoy the idea of descending. Many psychonavigators find a voyage into the depths to be most appealing. In Ceram, the Inner Pilot is visualized as a crocodile who leads people

down into the watery realms of the collective unconscious. Some practitioners like to descend into volcanos, lakes, or caves. Others prefer to ascend, rising high above a scene, like the Birdmen of the Andes. Some people prefer to visualize a linear journey, like the Shuara who are led by the jaguar across the floor of the jungle.

I prefer to feel myself rising. In my cross-legged position, I imagine that I am seated on a magic carpet. As I ascend, I watch with my mind's eye the objects around me—chairs, tables, walls—and slowly rise above them. I am able to pass through all the material things that are obstacles in the conscious world until I glide out into the air. Up and up I go. Looking down, I imagine the roof of my house and the street, and other buildings, moving faster, watching everything grow smaller and smaller. I quickly reach a point where I can look down and see nothing but mist. The earth is below me and I know that I can descend into any space I choose. I am not limited by space or time. Once there, I can contact my Inner Pilot.

An approach to this step that many find helpful is similar to one used in Surat Shabd Yoga ("The Path of the Masters"). The practitioner experiences himself or herself rising up toward the moon. Suddenly the moon splits in half; the practitioner passes between the two sections and heads on toward the sun and stars. The sun grows closer, the voyager rounds it and comes face-to-face with a Master. The Master then assumes the role of an Inner Pilot. In the words of Darshan Singh (an Indian business and political leader who was also an authority on Surat Shabd Yoga):

> [the Master] has taken me above body-consciousness, taken me with him to the higher planes, leaving the stars, the moon, and the sun behind, making me one with him in his radiant form, in his effulgent form. He has taken me into moments of eternity, beyond the limitations of time and space, and then given me a glance of love and a boost on the higher planes, he has taken me into the highest realms of spirituality. On the way he has introduced me to the various Masters who have blessed this earth since time immemorial, and arranged for our conversation.*

7. *Communicate with your Inner Pilot.* Inner Pilots can take many forms. Culture and religion often are instrumental and may determine

* Darshan Singh, *Spiritual Awakening* (Bowling Green, VA; Delhi, India: Sawan Kirpal Publications, 1986), pp 179–180.

what form your Inner Pilot will present. However, your own particular circumstances at any time may also influence the nature and appearance of your Inner Pilot. The following first-person accounts help to illustrate this. They are summaries of discussions I have had with people who psychonavigate.

Lisa, Artist:

I have three Inner Pilots. The one I call on most often is a man in his late twenties. Gruff looking, unshaven, not very handsome really, but kind. Whenever I'm having problems with a painting, I visit him. It starts off like meditation, but after awhile I see and feel myself moving into a land of fantastic trees, wild looking and vividly colored. Ivan—that's his name—meets me there. We've arranged a signal so I can be sure it's really him, not an imposter. He whistles a tune I loved as a kid.

I explain my problem to him. Actually, I don't usually understand it enough to explain it. I simply tell him about it. Next thing I know, I'm in the painting with him. We travel all around inside it. I learn a lot about my work, things I didn't understand before. It's an absolutely wonderful adventure, always. I've never been disappointed.

After our journey is over, I embrace him and thank him. He's very tender. Then, magically, I find myself in the beautiful forest again. When I go back to work on the painting, it is as though Ivan were there with me guiding my hand.

Ehud, President of a U.S. publishing company:

I experienced an encounter with an Inner Pilot during a vacation on the island of Majorca, off the coast of Spain. I had long wanted to visit the place where R.A. Schwaller de Lubicz and Raymond Lully had lived; the island where the Moors and Jews had found a last stronghold for their mystic practices during the Spanish Inquisition, before their final expulsion from the mainland. I was eager to be alone in Majorca's natural surroundings and, immediately after arriving, walked to the foot of a mountain near my hotel and began to climb.

It was late afternoon when I set out and, by the time I had climbed 3,000 feet to the summit, the sun was setting. As I looked out over the Mediterranean, I saw fast-moving storm clouds approaching. With unnerving speed they rolled in over the island, covering everything with a blanket of darkness. I knew I had to get off the mountain as quickly as possible and decided to forego the long, winding trail by which I'd come. Seeking the most direct line of descent (I could see the hotel from where I stood), I headed for a dense area of pine forest thick with underbrush. The terrain turned out to be dramatically rougher and steeper than what I'd encountered on my ascent, plus the increasing darkness was making it extremely difficult to see. I was no longer able to discern how far the ground extended or where a ledge might suddenly drop off; I felt as though I might fall right off the mountain face. To help steady myself I began moving on my hands and knees, close to the ground where the rocks and underbrush cut my flesh persistently.

I realized that it was treacherous to continue onward, and I seriously considered staying exactly where I was until morning, but I also knew that I was expected back at the hotel. If I didn't reappear sometime soon I was sure my friends would send the authorities out to look for me, causing a major disturbance. Trembling and in a state of near panic, I retreated into myself and prayed for guidance. Almost immediately an inner calm overtook me. When I opened my eyes I could dimly see a goat standing no more than a couple of yards away, facing directly toward me. In the same instant that it turned to walk away, the thought arose in my mind to follow. I moved very slowly and deliberately; the goat was not frightened of me in the least. Within a matter of minutes, the animal showed me the way to a clear path leading straight down the mountainside.

With a feeling of euphoria, I recalled the mythic significance of the goat as a representative of the pantheistic gods. It seemed that this guide had come from out of nowhere in answer to a genuine need, directing me out of my state of fear and entrapment to one of joyful liberation and abandonment.

Sarah, Environmental engineer for a U.S. construction company:

My grandfather was a road engineer. He helped design and build the Interstate Highway System. I spent a lot of time with him after he retired. We took walks in the forest behind his house. He taught me all about flowers, trees, birds, and the little animals we sometimes saw. When he died, I felt completely lost.

Now, I call on him often when I'm lonely, or if I need help

making decisions. In my job, a person can be overwhelmed with data. At decision time, it comes down to me. The data doesn't give answers, just information. Grandpa is always there when I call. I close my eyes and ask him to come, then I see him. He puts his arms around me and I feel his warm, loving, energy. His voice is soothing. I ask questions, and the things he says give me new insights.

I love him very much. He's the one who got me into this field, and helped me understand the importance of protecting our world. Now he keeps me honest, so to speak, and on the straight and narrow. I sometimes get a lot of pressure from project engineers and my boss to take short-cuts that could cause problems later. Grandpa gives me the courage I need to stand up to that pressure.

David, President of an international financial services company:

Every year for seventeen years now, I've spent at least a week in India studying with my master. I've learned to fly outside the bounds of consciousness, beyond time. An absolutely wonderful ability, one that's helped me more than I can say both in business and personally.

When I'm back in the states I can journey to a place high above, where I meet my master. He is an enlightened teacher who helps me through all sorts of problems. Perhaps more important even than this is the way he helps me see the world around me. I've come to appreciate things I never even noticed before: A flower outside my office, the lovely grain of a wood desk, the air I breathe. I realize that my job and my life are not just about making money and advising others how to do it; they're about enjoying the world I live in and making sure that it will be a world my daughter and her children can enjoy.

I don't talk much about this aspect of my life with clients and business associates unless I discover they are truly interested in such things. But it's amazing how many people I've met over the years who are interested. Our corporations are full of three-piece suited men and button-down women who fly beyond time. Well, "full" isn't the right word. There are many, but not enough. Every time another person joins our ranks, the world gets a little bit better.

Jim, Martial arts black belt:

Psychonavigation is very important. Before testing my skills, I use it to help me prepare, especially for breaking boards and cement blocks. I journey to a beautiful glen where I visit a Korean Master. He demonstrates the proper way. He does the breaks over and over in a kind of slow motion. And he helps me learn to focus my energy forces, my *chi*.

I was in a car accident and broke three toes. A real fluke! My wife and I had planned a ski vacation. The doctor said to forget it, there was no way I would heal in time. My Korean Master taught me how to travel inside my foot. I visualized an army of workers there. They were hammering, welding, drilling, and bolting my bones back together. Several times every day I took the journey. I watched them hard at work. I focussed my *chi* on those bones. And by God it worked! The bones mended in less than two months, and in time for our vacation. My doctor couldn't believe it.

Like many other psychonavigators, Jung understood that the process of entering the collective unconscious is a journey, one not lacking perils and false turns. He cultivated a number of Inner Pilots to help him find his way. Particularly vivid in his writings are the descriptions of an old man and a girl and his method for contacting them:

I frequently imagined a steep descent. I even made several attempts to get to very bottom. The first time I reached, as it were, a depth of about a thousand feet; the next time I found myself at the edge of a cosmic abyss. It was like a voyage to the moon, or a descent into empty space. First came the image of a crater, and I had the feeling that I was in the land of the dead. The atmosphere was that of the other world. Near the steep slope of a rock I caught sight of two figures, an old man with a white beard and a beautiful young girl. I summoned up my courage and approached them as though they were real people, and listened attentively to what they told me. . . .*

I have several different Inner Pilots. Some I call upon for help in specific areas, some are there for general guidance. At the moment, the most frequent is Manolo, a Quechua Indian who lives in an adobe hut beside an Andean lake ringed with volcanic peaks. He has helped me retell many of the incidents described in this book.

When I sit down to psychonavigate, sometimes I know which Inner Pilot I want to visit; I'll ask him or her to please come to me.

*Carl G. Jung, *Memories, Dreams, Reflections* (New York: Random House, 1965), p 181.

Often, however, I simply let myself go. A force I do not control takes me to the Andean lake, or to one of the other locations.

There is no secret to finding your Inner Pilot. Practice the steps outlined above, be open to what happens, and have faith. Don't get discouraged; it may take time. Keep trying. Many people draw upon their religion for help. Christians, for example, may find it easy to call upon Christ as their Inner Pilot.

8. *Return.* Once you have completed your journey, you are ready to return home. You will know when the time has arrived. Don't resist; there will be many more voyages to come. Thank your Inner Pilot. Tell him or her that you look forward to your next visit. Then return back, retracing the same route you used to arrive.

In my case, I shake hands with or embrace my Inner Pilot and share my feelings about our visit. I thank him or her and express my desire to meet again soon, promising to use whatever insights I have gained for the benefit of all concerned. Then I walk back to my magic carpet, sit cross-legged, and return in a reverse of the voyage described in step 6.

10

Posiguides

I have met many people who psychonavigate. For some, it is a relatively simple matter of holding discussions with inner guides. For others, it involves out-of-body experiences. Whatever the method, it helps unite mind, body, and soul. It is an integrating process that produces feelings of harmony. It allows us to reach vital parts of ourselves, and focus powerful energy reserves in areas where they are needed most. The more we practice it, the greater the benefits we receive.

If you want to psychonavigate and desire to have control over the process, you must have a positive attitude about yourself, and about life in general. There is no way around this requirement. This does not mean that negative thoughts will never enter your mind, or negative feelings your heart. It means that you should strive to overcome these. For success to be achieved, positive ideas and actions must predominate in the long run.

I find it helpful to remember four rules or guides. For convenience I refer to them as *Posiguides*. When I help people learn to psychonavigate, I suggest they write these guidelines down and tape them to their bathroom mirror or some other place where they will see them every day.

The four Posiguides are briefly stated and described below. They reflect principles discussed in earlier chapters.

Posiguide One: No matter what your situation, several times each day stop and think about the good aspects—the enjoyable and self-expanding ones—of what you are doing.

Every morning at breakfast, Teofilo Mata would anticipate the wonders of the coming day. "It's going to be a glorious day," he might say. Or he might walk to the door in the kitchen wall and look out over the Amazon at the rising sun. "Think of all the splendid possibilities today holds."

When you wake up in the morning, think about the day ahead and what new joys await you. You are alive, and this is your day. If you are in a situation which at first glance appears unappealing, concentrate on the opportunities to learn and expand your horizons. Realize that each task you do is special. Nothing is boring unless you allow yourself to perceive it as such. Focus on the positive, and greet the day with enthusiasm.

At mid morning, noon, and again in the late afternoon—think of what you have done so far. Focus on the joy of being alive and experiencing what you have done during the past few hours. Ask yourself how you might improve the situation, what you could do to increase your pleasure, and make a deal with yourself to do better in the coming hours.

I shall never forget my second visit to the Bugis' shipbuilding site. In the middle of all the frantic activity involved in repairing the defective prahu, Buli ambled over to us to apologize for not inviting us to lunch.

"Don't worry about us," I said. "You've got enough problems already."

He smiled gently. "Problems?" He spread his arms wide. "But it is a beautiful day. One for an old man to learn much."

For many adults, this attitude does not come automatically. Therefore, it is important that, at least at first, we set aside periods during the day to consciously think about it. Later, it will become part of our other levels of consciousness.

The time just before falling asleep provides another opportunity. You may find it helpful to review the day and give thanks for all the good things that happened. Try to see the positive facets in all events. Ones that seemed unpleasant or sad may have taught you valuable lessons, or created new opportunities. Focus on these aspects. Promise yourself that when you awake in the morning you will do so with an open heart, and with enthusiasm for the day to come.

Posiguide Two: Use visualization in a positive way; be aware throughout the day of the many times you visualize and take control of these; expunge your negative visions mercilessly and concentrate on positive ones.

We all visualize frequently. In fact, prior to doing almost anything, we visualize it. Before your hand reaches for a pencil, your mind visualizes the event. You see your hand reaching out and taking the pencil, then you do it. We have all experienced the passive movement into another stage of consciousness referred to as "daydreaming." Visualization, unlike daydreaming, is active. It can be controlled, and when it is, the process is highly creative.

Not surprisingly, visualization is a key to psychonavigation. It does not have to include more than one of the senses; however, the more senses that are involved, the more powerful it will be. When Julio and I meditated on the slopes of Pichincha, he taught me to incorporate smell, taste, sound, and touch into my visualizations. These lessons have proven extremely helpful during psychonavigation.

Visualization must always be combined with a positive attitude. When confronted with a problem, some of us tend to emphasize the negative. We may have established an unfortunate pattern of visualizing outcomes that are counterproductive to our goals or interests. Once these are fixed in our minds, we may focus on them and mull them over, worrying and fretting. We may wake up in the middle of the night, overcome with anxiety and "stressed out." Our bodies, minds, and spirits can be affected. All this helps reinforce and increase the momentum of the negative. Visualizing ways in which a situation may deteriorate gives energy to the negative. Ironically, we can set ourselves up, helping to assure that our worst fears will be realized.

The best lawyers exploit such negative visualizations. An attorney friend of mine once spelled this out clearly when he told me, "Half the battle is won the minute an adversary starts visualizing what life will be like after he loses. I've got him as soon as he allows the negative to invade his feelings. My first—and perhaps most important—job is to trigger his negative visions."

Such negatives must be swept from our minds. Expunge them mercilessly. Do not let people use you this way, and do not talk yourself into your own traps. Take control of your visualizations. See positive results that turn the negatives around. Have faith, and visualize the outcome you desire.

Visualization can be a highly effective tool. Take control of it; use it for positive results.

Posiguide Three: Attune yourself to nature, and understand what nature demonstrates so clearly—there is no such thing as failure.

We have learned that psychonavigating cultures see themselves as protectors of nature while technologically oriented cultures tend to view themselves as conquerors of nature. Nature reaffirms the positive aspects of life. It is the basis for everything. All life springs from nature, and ultimately returns to it. Einstein demonstrated that while exchanges may occur between matter and energy, there is continuity within nature. Matter and energy do not disappear. One may alter its form and become the other, and change back again to its original state. This may happen frequently; it may seem like an endless process. No matter how many times it happens, however, the basic continuity is not compromised.

Nature knows no failures, it evolves. Birth, life, and death are milestones along a continuum. There are outcomes, but no failures. Failure simply does not exist in nature.

People who live close to nature, those like the Shuara, Quechua, and Bugis who have not built technological doors to shut out their immediate environment, understand this fundamentally positive aspect of nature intimately. They do not view the world in terms of success and failure.

Don José Quischpe epitomized this outlook. Whenever I grew discouraged by the lack of success in finding markets for the co-op's bricks he would tell me to be patient. "Viracocha does not understand the word 'failure,'" he would say. Teofilo Mata expressed a similar viewpoint the morning he led me into his schoolhouse and told me that El Milagro would not end up with a credit and savings cooperative. Toyup, Buli, Yosuf, and many others since have echoed the same philosophy.

It took a long time for me to fully understand what these people were saying. At first, I accepted their attitude as an attempt to help relieve my burden of guilt. Eventually I came to understand that, in fact, it was based upon deep philosophical convictions. Viracocha does not have a word for failure because in nature failure does not exist.

Our modern technological cultures are among the very few in history that have defined events strictly in terms of success and failure. Perhaps this is not surprising, given that ours are also the cultures most alienated from nature. Failure and success are states of mind. They are perceptions, nothing more, nothing less.

When you attempt to bring forth your Inner Pilots, you may encounter resistance. Learn from this. You have not failed, you have moved farther along the learning curve. Take your cue from nature: There is no such thing as failure.

Posiguide Four: You have the ability to act and take control. As long as you realize this, how can you be anything but positive?

The idea that we are all created equal under God has been around for a long time. I think it means that we all have the power to act and control our inner destinies, even when our outer lives are limited by sickness, imprisonment, or other circumstances. At birth, we were granted free will. We have the power to change ourselves, our ideas, and our perceptions. No matter what happens, we can act.

This was a subject Julio often discussed. "I am saddened," he once told me, "to hear people say, 'oh, that's beyond my control;' or 'I do it because I have no choice.' I know these are unhappy people. They have elected to forego a god-given right. Why do they give up their power so easily?"

As we learned in *Posiguide Two*, negatives must be eradicated from our thinking. We each have the ability to act. Whenever we allow ourselves to think otherwise, we are encouraging the negative energy to build.

It is important for us to remember that, in fact, each of us is "the boss." One of the reasons we sometimes neglect to see ourselves as in control is because we do not really know what we want. We may say "I would like this," or "I would like that," but the truth is that we are not at all sure we really do want "this" or "that" enough to work for it. Therefore, we are reluctant to set goals and make and implement plans. Discouragement follows, along with the attitude of "I-can't-possibly-have-this-or-that."

When you find yourself in such a situation, remind yourself that you have the ability to act. You can obtain your goals. The only thing keeping you from it is your lack of desire, or your indecisiveness about your level of commitment.

"I love the jungle," Teofilo confided on the morning after Tanya and Bomi's visit. "It makes me feel free. I believe in what Jesus taught and in Virococha's philosophy. We are free—until and unless we convince ourselves otherwise. Even then we are still free. We just don't realize it. Here in the jungle, I know I'll never forget it. Look around. Everything here testifies to our freedom!"

We are in charge of our lives; we have the ability to act. Nothing we truly want is beyond our grasp, if we are willing to work hard enough for it. That is the message of psychonavigation. It is a message that is not aimed at any one of the legs of the mind-body-spirit triangle, but rather at all three taken as a whole. Hearing and understanding that message, how can we feel any way other than positive?

As a society, we have begun to realize that technology can bring the bad along with good. In our hearts we know that there is more to life than material advancement. History may well judge our fascination with the technical and material not only as folly, but also as the result of a deep cynicism and a rejection of values that sustained humankind for thousands of years. These positive values are the adhesive cementing body, mind, and spirit and sustaining cultures that live in cooperation with nature.

Today, we are faced with two diverging roads. We must choose one and move forward. The path behind us is history. Nothing will change what we have done. We have given ourselves marvelous devices; we also have depleted irreplaceable resources. We have poisoned our air, land, and water. Technology has both helped us and hurt us. We pause a moment, staring ahead, trying to find a clue. Which will be the road taken?

Perhaps, we begin to think as we study the fork in our path, it is not so much a matter of which road we select. Perhaps the real issue is us: our attitudes, our perceptions, what we see, smell, taste, and feel along the road, how well we listen, how we relate to the road, and what we choose to leave behind as we pass.

11

Manolo's Moon

In the early morning light I sit on a small carpet spread over the patio tile; my back rests comfortably against one of the pillars that supports our roof. I relax my body. I concentrate on the sound of the wind. My breathing slows. I enter the alpha state.

Slowly the carpet rises. On it, I glide out from under the roof and up toward the wisp of a cloud that is illuminated by a first ray of the still-unseen sun. Glancing down, I watch the patio fall away. I smell the scent of gardenias on the morning breeze. I sail swiftly over the neighborhood on my journey to another realm.

Up I travel, through a layer of clouds. Below, the earth rotates; it is a misty ball of splendid colors, resembling pictures beamed back by astronauts on their journey to the moon. The western bulge of South America lies directly underneath me.

I drop rapidly. In an instant, everything slows as if I've been transformed from a plummeting rock into a drifting leaf.

Suddenly I'm aware of mountains that are barely visible in the half light. Far away a solitary snow-capped peak juts high above the others. It captures a ray from the invisible sun and hurls it back. Nearer, the dark mountains form the rim of a bowl around a volcanic lake. I glide over the water toward a thatch-roofed adobe house.

Manolo steps through the door and walks towards me. He is short and barrel-chested like most Quechua. He wears a dark blue poncho, woolen pants, and an Incan knit cap with flaps hanging below his ears. A weathered hand is raised in greeting.

The carpet settles down beside him. I stand to shake his hand. "Manolo," I say, "it's good to see you."

He grasps my hand in one of his, and with the other embraces me. Together we walk up the slope toward the open door of his house. Breathing deeply, I smell the eucalyptus and wood smoke. This is home.

The inside of his house is dark. I can see only the wooden table and two chairs beside the doorway. "Sit down, John," he says. He waits for me, and then he too sits at the table.

"So . . ." he says.

"Manolo, I have a problem. I'm trying to write about 'soul wandering,' to explain how the spirit is able to leave the body, seek a thing—like the jaguar—and return to show the physical body the way there."

"Ah, yes, the Shuara."

"The Shuara, the Birdmen, the Bugis, you and me."

He smiles.

"We two are proof it works. But Manolo, I'm a businessman with clients and a reputation. How can I write about this so that it makes sense?"

"Yes." He places both hands on the table. "I understand." He pushes his chair back. The hard eucalyptus legs scrape noisily on the dirt floor. "In your own way, you're a shaman to your culture. We mustn't jeopardize your reputation. Follow me." Outside the light has not changed since we entered his house. A purple sky is speckled with stars. In the distance I glimpse the single sign of the coming day, the glint of sun reflected from the ice fields of that highest peak.

He leads me past the shadow of a mountain rising from the edge of the lake. I recall another day's conversations, when he taught me that the mountain is a source of inner power. "Sit next to it," he said. "Whenever you need strength, draw its energy into you." We pass the mountain and struggle up a winding trail. Our feet knock pebbles loose, sending them scuttling to the bottom. A few splash noisily into the lake.

At the top we look over the vast, silent Andes. There are mountains everywhere—jagged, ancient, enigmatic mountains. Many are blanketed in snow. But splendid as they are, my attention is drawn from them to the moon overhead. A bright moon, white and clear. I glance at Manolo. His head back, he sees the moon and the moon alone.

We stand there in silence. The moon is very close.

"She comes from the earth," he says, "from the great ocean to the west."

"I've heard that legend. The moon was ripped away from our planet millions of years ago. Gravity holds her like an umbilical cord."

"She has great power over things here on earth."

"You mean the tides?"

"The tides. The weather. Internal rhythms in people, animals, and plants. Power beyond our knowledge."

"Yes. I believe it."

I feel him turn towards me. My eyes meet his. His smile is gentle. "When our soul wanders, does it not leave the body like the moon left the earth? Does the soul not continue to exert power over our body even when it journeys?"

For a brief instant I see myself on the patio sitting on the carpet, my back leaning against a pillar. "Yes. Of course."

"Does it not send back messages about the course we should chart?"

I have to stop and think for a moment, recalling magazine covers and photos of the earth taken from the moon, a movie shown against an adobe wall. It seems to have happened long ago. . . . "When the astronauts landed on the moon, they—we—gained a whole new perspective. We came to realize how vulnerable we are, how self-contained, how small, and how limited are our resources. We used the expression 'spaceship earth' to describe this."

"And what does all this have to do with psychonavigation, John?"

"The soul wanders, finds the way, reads the guideposts, and comes back to tell the body how the guideposts work." He is watching me. "The body follows—may follow—the guideposts. To a jaguar or a distant island, to better health, the invention of the lightbulb, or the creation of a chapter in a book."

His eyes return to the moon. "Whether you follow those guide-posts or not is a choice left up to you."

I can think of nothing more to say. I stand there looking from him to the moon and back again. At long last, I speak the only words on my mind, "Mama Kilya."

"Sit down, please." I do as he requests. "Concentrate on the moon. See her. Touch her. Listen to her. Don't think only with your mind. Use your body and your spirit. Know where the moon came from, how she affects us, and what she has to say. If she can speak to your astronauts, surely she can speak to you."

I let my body relax. I try to empty myself of all distractions. As I concentrate on the moon, the silence is shattered by a chilling scream.

"My God! What was that?"

"What?"

"Didn't you hear it?" The sound takes me back to a night in El Milagro, before the earth turned to pottery. "Didn't you hear the scream of the jaguar?"

He gives me a strange look. "Jaguar? A jungle animal, John. Certainly you know that. There are none here."

"But I heard. . . ."

"Mama Kilya." He smiles.

The moon. It seems preposterous. A shadow glides across the silver orb, and again I hear the scream.

Manolo's head is nodding. "Yes," he says. "You heard Mama Kilya. She spoke to you. Now, what will you do about it?"

Bibliography

Alexander, F. *Psychosomatic Medicine*. New York: Norton, 1950.

Allison, J. Respiration changes during transcendental meditation. *Lancet* i (1970): 833-834.

Andrews, L. *Jaguar Woman and the Wisdom of the Butterfly Tree*. San Francisco: Harper & Row, 1986.

Bach, R. *Illusions: The Adventures of a Reluctant Messiah*. New York: Dell, 1977.

Benson, H. *Beyond the Relaxation Response*. New York: Times Books, 1984.

———. *The Relaxation Response*. New York: Morrow, 1975.

Blair, L., with Blair, L. *Ring of Fire: Exploring the Last Remote Places of the World*. New York: Bantam Books, 1988.

Bower, B. Shaping up your mind. *Science News* 126(August 2, 1986): 75.

Buscaglia, L. *The Way of the Bull*. New York: Ballantine Books, 1983.

Castaneda, C. *The Eagle's Gift*. New York: Simon and Schuster, 1981.

Castaneda, C. *The Teachings of Don Juan: A Yaqui Way of Knowledge*. Los Angeles: University of California Press, 1968.

Chan, W. *A Source Book in Chinese Philosophy*. Princeton, N.J.: Princeton University Press, 1963.

Chang, C. Y. *Creativity and Taoism*. New York: Julian Press, 1963.

Chatwin, B. *The Songlines*. New York: Penguin Books, 1988.

Colby, N. and Colby, L. *The Daykeeper*. Cambridge, Ma.: Harvard University Press, 1981.

Crichton, M. *Travels*. New York: Alfred A. Knopf, 1988.

Dossey, L. *Space, Time and Medicine*. Boston: New Science Library, 1982.

Fisher, R. A cartography of the ecstatic and meditative states. *Science* 174(1971): 897-904.

Gartelmann, K. *Digging Up Prehistory: The Archaeology of Ecuador.* Quito: Ediciones Libri Mundi, 1986.

Herdt, G. *Guardians of the Flutes: Idioms of Masculinity.* New York: Columbia University Press, 1987.

Holmes, T. H., and Rahe, R. H. The social readjustment rating scale. *Journal of Psychosomatic Research* II(1967): 213.

Jacobson, E. *Progressive Relaxation.* Chicago: University of Chicago Press, 1938.

James, E. *Attaining the Mastership: Advanced Studies on the Spiritual Path.* Atlanta: Dhamma Books, 1988.

Jana, H. Energy metabolism in hypnotic trance and sleep. *Journal of Applied Physiology* 20(1965): 308-310.

Johnston, W. *Christian Zen.* New York: Harper & Row, 1971.

Jung, C. *Memories, Dreams, Reflections.* New York: Vintage Books, 1961.

Kaplan, J. Pressure points...Active answers. *Vogue* (August 1987): 353.

Katkin, H. S., and Murray, E. N. Instrumental conditioning of autonomically mediated behavior: Theoretical and methodological issues. *Psychological Bulletin* 70(1968): 52-68.

Kühlewind, G. *Stages of Consciousness: Meditations on the Boundaries of the Soul.* New York: Inner Traditions and Stockbridge, Ma.: Lindisfarne Press, 1984.

Laszlo, E. *Introduction to Systems Philosophy—Toward a New Paradigm of Contemporary Thought.* Foreword by Ludwig von Bertalanffy. New York: Harper Torchbooks, 1973.

Lawlor, R. *Earth Honoring: The New Male Sexuality.* Rochester, Vt.: Park Street Press, 1989.

LeShan, L. *How to Meditate.* New York: Little, Brown, 1974.

Lidell, L., Rabinovitch, N., and Rabinovitch, G. *The Sivananda Companion to Yoga.* New York: Simon and Schuster, 1983.

Luthe, W., ed. *Autogenic Therapy,* Vols. 1-5. New York: Grune and Stratton, 1969.

May, R. *The Courage To Create.* New York: Norton, 1975.

McIntyre, L. *The Incredible Incas and their Timeless Land.* Washington, D.C.: National Geographic Society, 1975.

McKenna, M. *Revitalize Yourself! The Techniques of Staying Youthful.* New York: Hawthorn Books, 1972.

Monroe, R. *Journeys Out of the Body.* New York: Doubleday, 1971.

Moss, G. E. *Illness, Immunity, and Social Interaction: The Dynamics of Biosocial Resonation.* New York: 1973.

Naranjo, C., and Ornstein, R. E. *On the Psychology of Meditation.* New York: Viking Press, 1971.

Needleman, J. *The New Religions.* Garden City, N.Y.: Doubleday, 1970.

Organ, T. W. *The Hindu Quest for the Perfection of Man.* Athens, Ohio: Ohio University Press, 1970.

Ornstein, R. E. *The Psychology of Consciousness.* San Francisco: W. H. Freeman, 1972.

Perkins, J. *The Stress-Free Habit: Powerful Techniques for Health and Longevity from the Andes, Yucatan, and Far East.* Rochester, Vt.: Healing Arts Press, 1989.

Pilkington, R. Cyberphysiology in children. *Advances: Journal of the Institute for the Advancement of Health,* Vol. 5, No. 4(1988), 66-69.

Scotch, N. A. Sociocultural factors in the epidemiology of Zulu hypertension. *American Journal of Public Health and the Nation's Health* 53(1963): 1205-1213.

Sheldrake, R. *A New Science of Life: the Hypothesis of Formative Causation.* Los Angeles: Jeremy P. Tarcher, Inc., 1987.

Singh, D. *Spiritual Awakening.* Bowling Green, Va.: Sawan Kirpa Publications, 1986.

Slocum, J. *Sailing Alone Around the World.* New York: Dover Publications, 1956.

Spalding, B. *Life & Teachings of the Masters of the Far East,* Vols. 1-3. Marina Del Rey, Ca.: DeVorss & Co., 1944.

Triminham, J. S. *Sufi Orders in Islam.* Oxford: Clarendon Press, 1971.

Villoldo, A. and Krippner, S. *Healing States (A Journey into the World of Spiritual Healing and Shamanism).* New York: Simon & Schuster, 1987.

Van Hagen, V. *The Ancient Sun Kingdoms of the Americas.* London: Thames & Hudson, 1962.

Wakefield, C. *High Cities of the Andes.* San Carlos, Ca.: Wide World Publishing/Tetra, 1988.

Wallace, R. K. Physiological effects of transcendental meditation. *Science* 167(1970): 1751-1754.

Wallace, R. K., and Benson, H. The physiology of meditation. *Scientific American* 226(1972): 84-90.

Wood, C. Herpes: Think positive. *Psychology Today* (December 1986): 24.

———. Relaxation really works. *Psychology Today* (January 1987): 68.

Index

Acknowledgments

I wish to give special thanks to Ehud Sperling for his insights and the encouragement he has offered me, and to Leslie Colket for her dedication, her willingness to share her writing skills, and especially her perseverance as an editor.

For additional information on psychonavigation and ways to visit psychonavigating cultures in Asia and Latin America, please write to:

John Perkins
P.O. Box 31357
Palm Beach Gardens FL 33420